INTRODUCTION

The purpose of this readers' guide is to help researchers to find their way into the nineteenth century census returns held by the Public Record Office (PRO). Whether they are seeking to compare occupations in a particular suburb of an industrial town over a thirty-year period, or to search for an individual in the course of piecing together a family history, it will give them guidance in understanding and interpreting this significant and fascinating source. It explains how to cope with the census reading rooms at the Public Record Office, and how to use the PRO's finding aids to identify the relevant microfilm (the medium by which these records are made available). It should be of value to those consulting census microfilms held outside the PRO, in local record offices and libraries, because it clarifies the structure of the census and also deals with a variety of problems encountered by its readers (eg how to locate a particular place or to seek a missing house).

The ideal enumerator

'A person of intelligence and activity, he must read and write well and have some knowledge of arithmetic. He must not be infirm or of such weak health as may render him unable to undergo the requisite exertion. He should not be younger than 18 years or older than 65 years. He must be temperate, orderly and respectable and be such a person as is likely to conduct himself with strict propriety and deserve the good will of the inhabitants of his district.'

The ideal householder

'The schedule should be received with intelligent acquiescence, and filled up with the persuasion that the integrity and enlightenment of all are tacitly challenged to take a conscientious share fulfilling a truly important duty.'

The Caernarfon and Denbigh Herald, 1871

MAKING USE OF THE CENSUS

BY

SUSAN LUMAS

PRO Publications

ACKNOWLEDGEMENTS

Thanks are due to many people who helped with the compilation of this guide. Evelyn Goode input the text initially and subsequently took it through its many drafts to what you see before you. Melvyn Stainton was responsible for the painstaking transformation from typescript to illustrated book. I also owe a debt to many colleagues who have shared my enthusiasm for the Victorian censuses and who have sat behind the census room enquiry desk at one time or another: Joe Saunders, who taught me all I know; Andy Bodle, Nigel Kent and Gerry Toop, who contributed helpful advice; Amanda Bevan, Mandy Banton, John Post, David Crook, Elizabeth Hallam-Smith and Alfred Knightbridge, who guided a rough draft through many editorial metamorphoses to its present state; Hugh Ashley Rayner, who photographed the documents; and especially Edward Higgs, whose much greater knowledge of how and why the census was taken was always there to be tapped when necessary. Thanks are also due to the late Alan Reed who provided some useful information based on his considerable experience as a lecturer on the subject and, last but not least, to all those searchers, record agents and transcribers who pointed out interesting entries, who shared their experience and who asked the questions.

The provenance and date of the cover illustration are unknown. It is likely that it was used in a newspaper to publicise the imminent taking of the census.

PRO Publications,
Public Record Office, Chancery Lane,
London WC2A 1LR

Crown copyright 1993
Second Edition
ISBN 1 873162 05 7

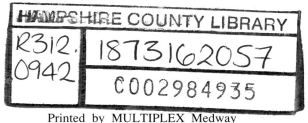
Printed by MULTIPLEX Medway

CONTENTS

ILLUSTRATIONS

MAKING USE OF THE CENSUS

The nineteenth century census returns provide a fascinating field of study and a valuable introduction to the use of archives. Many people might not need to look at original documents until their studies point them first in the direction of the enumerators' returns and all they have to offer; but they will soon find that the returns provide a rich source for many areas of research: from general population studies of an economic or social nature, through research into particular localities, to studies of individuals by family historians and biographers. It is not possible, however, just to walk into a reading room to find an index designed for your exact purpose that will lead you straight to the particular page, or pages, of the census returns that you require. Archives are left in the order in which they remained after their immediate administrative use was over, which tells us something of how they were compiled and administered. They have not been rearranged to suit the potential user, because today's researcher may not be seeking the same information as a reader of one hundred years hence.

WHAT THERE IS AND WHERE TO FIND IT

A census of Great Britain has been taken every decade from 1801 onwards, with the exception of 1941 when war intervened. The results were digested and published as Parliamentary Papers, to provide population counts (see appendix 1) and other social statistics for immediate use. For a detailed study of how and why the census was taken see E J Higgs, *Making Sense of the Census* (see bibliography appendix 13).

The earlier returns, for 1801 to 1831, were simply a numerical count and give little detailed information except where an enumerator decided to exceed his duties and include more. These returns have not been officially preserved but some survive locally, often in county record offices. The whereabouts of such survivals may be discovered by consulting J S W Gibson's *Marriage, Census and other Indexes for Family Historians*, and C R Chapman's *Pre 1841 Censuses and Population Listings*.

From 1841, however, all the enumerators' returns, but not the original schedules, have been officially preserved in theory, although in practice not all have survived. It was realised that these returns could usefully serve purposes other than those intended by the original survey.

The returns for England and Wales, which include the Isle of Man and the Channel Islands (referred to as Islands in the British Seas), the Isle of Wight (returned with Hampshire), and the Scilly Isles (returned with Cornwall), for 1841 to 1891 (HO 107, RG 9 to RG 12)

HM Napoleon III Emperor of the French RG 10/876, f 14 p 82

are available on microfilm, and for 1891 also on microfiche, for public inspection at the Public Record Office in Chancery Lane, London WC2A 1LR (telephone 081 876 3444 extension 2602). The census reading rooms are open between 9.30 am and 5.00 pm on weekdays.

Copies are also available in some local record offices and libraries (see J S W Gibson's *Census Returns 1841 - 1881 on Microfilm*). In the United States of America, copies on microfilm of all returns are held by The Genealogical Society of Utah, 50 East North Temple, Salt Lake City, Utah 84150.

The returns are, however, subject to a one hundred year closure period because of the personal information which they contain. One hundred years means one hundred years, not ninety-nine years and a half; the census returns, having usually been taken in April, are opened after their closure period on the first working day of the following year. For the dates of census night for each year see appendix 1.

The 1901 census for England and Wales, which is still in the custody of the Registrar General, may be consulted for information on a person's age and place of birth only, if you are a direct descendant of the individual or individuals whose details you require, or next of kin, where the person has died childless, by applying (on form CAS 1/C) to the General Register Office, St Catherine's House, 10 Kingsway, London WC2B 6JP, for a search to be made. Because of the stricter assurances of confidentiality than for earlier censuses given at that time it is not yet possible to do the same for 1911. Also the returns for that year were not entered into enumerators' books, so a search of the original schedules which are retained in place of the books would present considerable difficulties.

The Scottish returns are held at the General Register Office for Scotland, New Register House, Edinburgh EH1 3YT (telephone 031 556 395).

Irish returns rarely survive before 1901. *Handbook on Irish Genealogy,* published by Heraldic Artists Ltd., Dublin lists, on p 39, those census records which have survived in the National Archives in Dublin for some counties. Begley's *Irish Genealogy: A Record Finder* (p 51), has a comprehensive survey of Irish census returns from as far back as 1630 to 1981, and a full list of what has survived. These two lists are not identical.

Censuses were also taken in many British colonies on the same dates as those for the UK, but little information other than the purely statistical exists for them in this country. There is, however, a census of convicts in New South Wales and Tasmania, 1788 to 1859, in HO 10/21-27; an 1811 census of Surinam (CO 278/15-25); a 1715 census of Barbados but only of the white population (CO 28/16); and a census of Sierra Leone for 1831 (CO 267/111).

John Cadbury Cocoa Manufacturer   RG 9/2124, f 4 p 2

ARRANGEMENT OF THE RECORDS

The census returns are arranged topographically (that is, by place) in the order in which they appear in the published tables. The arrangement follows the system used for the registration of births, marriages and deaths. In 1836, when civil registration was established, the poor law unions were used as a foundation for the boundaries of the registration districts. The superintendent registrar's districts, grouped into eleven divisions, were also used as administrative units for census taking and were numbered. The divisions are described in appendix 2. The returns appear in numerical order of registration district. Later legislation altered the boundaries of the superintendent registrar's districts in order to confine individual districts within county boundaries which hitherto some had straddled. Some places, therefore, moved from one district to another as later censuses were taken. See appendix 7 for a complete list of registration districts and their numbers.

Each superintendent registrar's district is divided into sub-districts, and each sub-district into enumeration districts. The enumeration districts vary in size. Those covering a rural area took into account the distance that one man could travel in a day to collect the schedules from each household. On the other hand, enumeration districts in large towns, with a greater concentration of people, cover a much smaller area on the ground but a much larger number of individuals. Parishes, townships, tithings, hamlets and liberties are gathered into appropriate enumeration districts, which may consist of several small places or an entire parish. In other cases there may be several enumeration districts covering one large parish. It is important to remember that these parishes are civil parishes and do not necessarily have the same boundaries as their ecclesiastical equivalents.

The civil parish was the result of poor law administration which in itself created boundary problems. The ecclesiastical parishes, which were based on the ancient parishes of England and Wales together with chapelries created when the population increased and needed more places of worship, were found to be too large and unwieldy for administrative purposes and individual townships or tithings and villages were allowed to levy their own rates. This resulted in the establishment of civil parishes, as distinct from ecclesiastical districts or parishes, especially during the nineteenth century. In 1871 the ancient parishes which had not already been sub-divided into chapelries and townships were renamed as civil parishes. In addition there were extra-parochial places called liberties, or simply termed extra-parochial. All of these sub-divisions are mentioned in the population tables; the ecclesiastical districts are in separate sections at the end of each region. For census searching, however, ecclesiastical districts are usually ignored and the civil parish is the unit which matters.

James A H Murray Lexicographer RG 12/1166 , f 65 p 3

HOW THE CENSUS WAS TAKEN

In the week preceding census night (see appendix 1 for the date of each census) the appointed enumerator delivered schedules (see pp 7 and 8) to all the households in the area to which he had been assigned. The schedule was a form that every householder was obliged to complete. A householder was anyone who rented or owned a dwelling, a lodger being a householder if he or she lived in the same building but had separate accommodation from the rest of the people living there. A boarder was someone who lived with the householder's family and shared their dining table, unlike a lodger who occupied a separate household (see p 55) for a boarder and a lodger under one roof). Everyone who slept in the house on census night was to be included, even if it was not their permanent home. The instructions to the enumerator were that no person present on that night was to be omitted, and no person absent included. If individuals were working that night, or were travelling, they would be enumerated in the house to which they would normally return on the morning after they had finished their shift, or where they were to stay at the next stop on their journey.

On the Monday after the census night the enumerator returned to collect the completed schedules. If any had not been filled in, the enumerator had to do so by asking the householder for the information.

> *ENUMERATOR'S REMARKS FROM 1851 CENSUS FOR LONDON*
>
> *ALL HALLOWS, BARKING, LONDON*
>
> *The enumeration of this district was undertaken by me in the belief that I should be fairly paid for my services.*
>
> *I was not aware that all the particulars were to be entered by the enumerator in a book, the work without that, being ample for the sum paid, nor had I any idea of the unreasonable amount of labour imposed. The distribution, collection etc of the schedules together with the copying of the same occupied from two or three hours for every sixty persons enumerated, and for that - the equivalent is - ONE SHILLING!!!*
>
> *What man possessing the intelligence and business habits necessary for the undertaking would be found to accept it, if aware of the labour involved. How then can a correct return of the population be expected?*
>
> *He who proposed the scale of remuneration, should, in justice, be compelled to enumerate a large district, such as this upon the terms he had himself fixed.*
>
> *HO 107/1531, f 193*

John Poyntz, Earl and Groom to the Prince Consort RG 9/949, f 32 p 19

CENSUS OF ENGLAND AND WALES, 1871.

No. 14.

HOUSEHOLDER'S SCHEDULE.

Prepared under the direction of one of Her Majesty's Principal Secretaries of State, pursuant to the Act of 33 and 34 Vict., c. 107.

TO THE OCCUPIER.

This Paper will be CALLED FOR on **MONDAY, APRIL 3rd,** by the appointed Enumerator.

GEORGE GRAHAM, *Registrar General.*

Approved
H. A. BRUCE.
Home Office, Whitehall, Nov. 17th, 1870.

GENERAL INSTRUCTION.

This Paper to be filled up by the OCCUPIER or person in charge of the dwelling.

If a house is let or sub-let to separate Families or Lodgers, each OCCUPIER or LODGER must make a return for his portion of the house upon a SEPARATE PAPER.

INSTRUCTIONS for filling up the Column headed "RANK, PROFESSION, or OCCUPATION."

A person following more Distinct Occupation than one, should insert them in the order of their importance.

THREE EXAMPLES of the MODE OF FILLING UP THE HOUSEHOLDER'S SCHEDULE.

	Name and Surname.	Relation to Head of Family.	Condition.	Sex.	Age (last Birthday).	Rank, Profession, or Occupation.	Where Born.	If (1) Deaf-and-Dumb (2) Blind (3) Imbecile or Idiot (4) Lunatic.
1st Example								
1	George Wood	Head of Family	Married	M.	48	Farmer of 317 acres, employing 8 labourers and 3 boys	Surrey, Godstone	
2	Maria Wood	Wife	Married	F.	44	Farmer's Wife	Scotland	
3	Alan Wood	Son	Unmarried	M.	20	Farmer's Son	Surrey, Godstone	
4	Flora Jane Wood	Daughter		F.	12	Scholar	Kent, Ramsgate	
5	Ellen Wood	Mother	Widow	F.	71	Annuitant	Middlesex, Paddington	
6	Eliza Edwards	Servant	Unmarried	F.	24	General Servant (Domestic)	Surrey, Croydon	
7	Ann Young	Servant	Unmarried	F.	24	Dairymaid	Essex, Epping	
8	Thomas Jones	Servant	Unmarried	M.	21	Farm Servant		Lunatic
2nd Example								
1	Janet Cox	Head of Family	Widow	F.	43	Staymaker	Scotland	Blind from Small pox
2	William Cox	Son	Unmarried	M.	14	Basket-maker	Surrey, Lambeth	
3	Sophia Cox	Daughter	Unmarried	F.	24	Dressmaker	Middlesex, Poplar	
4	Alexander Cox	Grandson		M.	11 months		Middlesex, Shoreditch	
5	Margaret Cox	Mother-in-law	Widow	F.	73	Formerly Laundress	Ireland	
6	John Butler	Boarder	Widower	M.	42	Printer—Compositor	France (British Subject)	
3rd Example								
1	Walter Johnson	Lodger	Unmarried	M.	23	Ship Carpenter	Durham, Sunderland	

BY AUTHORITY:—Ford and Tilt, Long Acre, London, Printers to Her Majesty's Stationery Office.

Householder's schedule for Victoria Street, Sheffield RG 10/4677, f 76

Completed schedule for the Wrangham family RG 10/4677, f 76

The schedules were then copied by the enumerator into a book (several of which were bound together into folders) and handed in to the registrar who checked that everything was satisfactory.

SUPERINTENDENT REGISTRAR'S DISTRICT.		Area in Statute Acres.	HOUSES.						POPULA		
			1851.			1861.			Persons.		Mal
SUB-DISTRICT.	Parish, Township, or Place.		Inha-bited.	Un-inha-bited.	Build-ing.	Inha-bited.	Un-inha-bited.	Build-ing.	1851.	1861.	1851.
495. TODMORDEN.											
1. HEBDEN BRIDGE	*Halifax, part of* Parish —[a]										
	Wadsworth - - Township	10080	957	166	–	923	158	2	4491	4141	2188
	Erringden - - Township	2980	583	47	1	371	44	–	2004	1764	995
	Heptonstall - -[aa] Township	5320	882	127	2	790	170	6	4177	3497	2017
	Stansfield, *part of* • -[aa] Township [viz., the Lower Third Division.]		553	95	3	320	98	2	1790	1424	901
2. TODMORDEN -	*Halifax, part of* Parish—[a]	5920									
	Stansfield, *part of* • - Township [viz., the Middle Third and Upper Third Division.]		1152	102	11	1351	62	16	5837	6750	2923
	Langfield - - Township	2620	752	41	55	890	35	10	3729	4391	1803
	Rochdale, part of Parish—[b]										
	TODMORDEN and Walsden (*Lancashire*) - - Townp.	–	1481	114	31	1790	67	57	7699	9146	3753
496. SADDLEWORTH.											
1. DELPH [bb] - -	Saddleworth, *part of* † - Township (*part of Rochdale* Parish.[b])	18280	1819	230	10	2048	169	11	9440	9754	4647
2. UPPER MILL [bb] -	Saddleworth, *part of* (W) † Township (*part of Rochdale* Parish.[b])		1548	105	18	1770	116	6	8359	8877	4190
497. HUDDERSFIELD.											
1. SLAITHWAITE -	*Huddersfield, part of* Parish—[c]										
	Slaithwaite - - Township	2320	553	29	7	575	11	2	2852	2932	1460
	Marsden { in *Huddersfield* Parish [c] -	2050	103	9	6	138	14	–	512	662	273
	Tnp.‡ [d] { in *Almondbury* Parish § [e] -	5061	407	50	4	428	23	1	2153	2027	1091
	Almondbury, part of Parish—§ [e]										
	Lingards - - Township	500	159	4	–	149	4	–	811	783	405
	Linthwaite, *part of* ‖ - [f] Township	809	264	13	–	309	16	2	1355	1567	692
2. MELTHAM -	*Almondbury, part of* Parish—§ [e]										
	South Crosland - Township	1560	536	36	2	582	38	5	2784	2794	1392
	Meltham - - Township	4525	684	42	20	795	75	2	3758	4046	1794
3. HONLEY -	*Almondbury, part of* Parish—§ [e]										
	Honley (W) - [g] Township	2790	1077	35	17	987	186	3	5595	4626	2775
	Netherthong - - Township	850	228	13	5	223	30	–	1207	1097	615
4. HOLMFIRTH	*Almondbury, part of* Parish—§ [e]										
	Upperthong - -[gg] Township	710	459	22	7	543	21	2	2463	2690	1235
	Austonley - -[ee] Township	1760	373	18	4	363	38	–	2234	1901	1130
	Holme - - Township	3990	140	1	2	141	13	–	849	807	451
	Kirkburton, part of Parish—¶ [h]										
	Cartworth, *part of* ** - [i] Township	–	446	19	6	456	51	1	2298	2249	1168
	Wooldale, *part of* †† - [i] Township	–	657	36	11	668	54	–	3469	3198	1804
5. NEWMILL -	*Kirkburton, part of* Parish—¶ [h]										
	Wooldale, *part of* †† - [i] Township	2370	393	26	8	411	80	2	2131	2124	1070
	Cartworth, *part of* ** - [i] Township	2820	47	10	–	47	1	–	240	254	118
	Hepworth - - Township	3370	270	15	2	276	23	–	1532	1530	795
	Fulstone - - Township	1200	415	10	3	455	43	–	2257	2414	1177

The books were then sent to the census office in Craig's Court, London where they were checked again. Finally, when all the information had been analysed it was published as a Parliamentary Paper in the form of a series of tables relating to various subjects and the original schedules were destroyed. The tables most used by searchers are the tables of population arranged by registration districts (see bibliography appendix 13). Copies are available in the Census Room on request.

From 1891 women too could act as enumerators; it will be interesting to see how many accepted the challenge (see p 54).

Henry Mackeson   Alderman Brewer   HO 107/1633, f 543   p 1

THE CENSUS ROOM

On arrival at the Public Record Office, Chancery Lane, you will be directed to the Census Room in the basement by signs along the entrance corridor. You will be allowed access by signing your name in the register; you will need a reader's ticket only if you intend to visit the other Chancery Lane reading rooms. When you sign the book you will be given a numbered pass to hang round your neck. This allows you into the rooms and indicates where you find your seat by the number found in front of one of the microfilm readers. When you reach the Census Room you will see that it is a series of interconnecting rooms - a plan is in appendix 5.

You come first to a cloakroom where you can leave your coat and excess baggage. Handbags larger than 10" x 7" x 3" are not allowed into any of the reading rooms. The Office will not accept responsibility for loss or damage to personal property, so please watch any possessions taken in with you.

Next proceed along the corridor, passing on your left two rooms that have been set aside for eating and drinking when you need a break. At the far end of the corridor you will find the series of interconnecting rooms that together make up the Census Room.

When you arrive you will be assigned a seat number (it is printed on the back of the day pass you are handed at the reception desk). Before you find your seat, however, you need to consult the books in the reference rooms.

The first three rooms through the double doors are the reference rooms which provide you with all the information you need to identify the specific reels of film necessary for your search. See appendix 4 for the layout of the reference rooms.

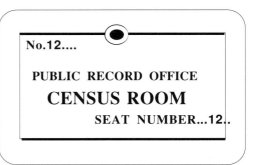

Gabriel Rozetti Professor of Italian HO 107/12493, f 130 p 13

The first of the three rooms contains the drawers which hold the 1891 films, the surname indexes and International Genealogical Index (IGI), with microfiche readers and some street directories. In the filing cabinets you will find a set of nearly all the published surname indexes, arranged by registration district number. These have been compiled by family history societies who often regard the Public Record Office, Society of Genealogists and the Genealogical Library at Salt Lake City as a place of deposit; PRO staff are always pleased to receive them. In the second room you will see the finding aids which will help you identify the microfilm you need to consult. These are grouped by census year and bound in different colours; 1841 in green, 1851 in red, 1861 in blue, 1871 in brown, 1881 in cream and 1891 in white. They are described in greater detail below on page 13 but are summarised here. There are enquiries desks in the first and third of these reference rooms should you need any help.

On the shelves, grouped by the years of the census, you will find:

An index to places
A class list which gives you the film references (also called a reference book)
Street indexes to London and other large towns

On another set of shelves is a collection of further miscellaneous finding aids which help if any queries arise. They are:

copies of London street directories for the
    census years (also with colour-coded bindings)
three volumes that locate London streets
a list of ecclesiastical parishes
an index to 1861 shipping
an index to hamlets
an 1854 map of London

Additionally, at the officer's desk there are five volumes which help clarify the whereabouts of London streets and a volume that explains the changes in county boundaries and civil parishes during the nineteenth century. Finally, there is an alphabetical index to registration districts which gives a list of churches and chapels in each.

Thomas Boozey Music Publisher HO 107/662, book 4 f 9 p 9

The PRO also makes available, on microfiche, a copy of the International Genealogical Index to enable people with an interest in individuals to ascertain in which county or counties a particular name is dominant. Once a successful search has been made for a family or an individual, a glance at the IGI will enlarge a searcher's knowledge of the spread of a particular surname in the county of birthplaces found in the census. It may even lead you to the specific reference in a parish or nonconformist register, as the IGI is an index to all the nonconformist registers held at the PRO and to many parish registers or parts of parish registers from all over the country.

The section on finding aids which follows explains in more detail how to use the reference rooms. They are a self-service operation although the staff are there to assist should you get into difficulties.

Beyond the reference rooms there is another room where you may obtain photocopies of successful searches. This is a self-service facility: see p 58 and p 59 which show you how to use a reader-printer and p 57 describing how to identify the particular part of the film you wish to copy.

In the autumn of 1993 some of these finding aids will be moved to decrease the amount of congestion. The intended layout of the reference and photocopy area is shown in appendix 5.

The PRO does not permit children under eleven years old to enter the Census Room. Children of eleven years and over are allowed in the Census Room only if they are searching the returns themselves and not just accompanying an adult who is doing so.

Drinking, eating and the chewing of gum are forbidden in all parts of the Census Room. When you need a break, please eat and drink in the separate waiting room provided. Smoking is forbidden throughout the building.

William Wisden   Cricket Outfitter RG 11/1088, f 16 p 25

USING THE REFERENCE ROOM

To select a microfilm of the part of the census returns you wish to see, you need its reference number (see appendix 6 for a full explanation of reference numbers). To determine this you need to look at one or more reference books, known as finding aids. The books are all clearly labelled by year and contents and are bound in different colours according to the year of the census (see above p 11). They are:

    1 Place-name indexes
    2 Class lists
    3 London street indexes
    4 Country street indexes
    5 Surname indexes
    6 Additional finding aids
        i)   An index to London streets
        ii)   An index to abolished London street names
        iii)   Shipping index
        iv)   List of ecclesiastical parishes
        v)   Hamlet index
        vi)   List of churches and chapels
        vii)   London street directories
        viii) Maps
        ix)   Population tables
        x)   Miscellaneous topographical indexes

The census returns, as explained above (p 5), are arranged in numerical order of the superintendent registrar's districts. This presupposes that you know in which order they are numbered so that you can find your way around the country. Once into your registration district you need to know which sub-district contains your place, and so on. Each set of census returns has an index to place names based on the index provided with the printed population tables. This is insufficient, however, when searching large towns, where it is totally impractical to read every frame on the film in the hope of finding the information you seek. Places with a population of over 40,000 have, therefore, been provided with a street index to take you to the correct folios of the enumerator's returns. These street indexes are provided by the PRO. Appendixes 8-12 list all the places covered for each census year.

To search the returns, therefore, you have three options at the outset. If you want to look at a small village or town, consult the place-name index and then the class list (see 1 and 2 below). Alternatively, if you are searching a large town with a population of over 40,000 (then, not now), you need a street index to narrow your search (see 3 and 4 below). If you are looking for an individual, however, especially in 1851, you may find that there is a surname index to your district (see 5 below).

Benjamin Disraeli Independent HO 107/733, book 14 f 45 p 14

```
        PLACE NAME INDEX FOR 1841 CENSUS RETURNS
                             COUNTY          REF.BOOK
           PLACE NAME        ABBREV.         PAGE NUMBER
Elmstead                    Essex                90
Elmstead                    Kent                144
Elmsthorpe                  Leics               172
Elmstone                    Kent                139
Elmstone Hardwicke          Glos             96,103
Elmstree                    Glos                100
Elmton                      Derb                 52
Elm, Little                 Som                 303
Elm, North                  Som                 301
Elsdon                      Northumb            249
Elsdon Ward                 Northumb            249
Elsecar                     Yorks WR            449
Elsenham                    Essex                91
Elsey                       Lincs               193
Elsfield                    Oxon                269
Elsham                      Lincs               187
Elsing                      Norf                224
Elslack                     Yorks WR            440
Elson                       Salop               291
Elstead                     Surrey              342
Elsted                      Sussex              350
Elsthorpe                   Lincs               177
Elstob                      Durh                 82
Elston                      Lancs               151
Elston                      Notts            264,267
Elston                      Wilts               377
Elstow                      Beds                  2
Elstree                     Herts               130
Elstree                     Midd                203
Elstronwick                 Yorks ER            398
Elstub                      Wilts               377
Elswick                     Lancs  |1841|       151
Elswick                     North|              247
Elsworth                    Cambs                17
```

1 PLACE-NAME INDEXES

The indexes of place names include the names of registration districts and of every other smaller division.

The index to places for 1841 gives you a page number to go to in the class list (see 2 below). Place indexes for other years simply give you the name and number of the registration district in which that place occurs and, since the class lists are arranged in numerical order of registration district, it is a quick process to go from the place-name index to the class list in order to obtain the reference you need to identify your reel of film.

New place-name indexes, to show not just the registration district number but also whether there is a street index and a surname index available for each particular place, are now on the shelves of the reference room. When you look up your place in the place-name index you will discover the number of the registration district in which it can be found. This registration district number is repeated in the street index and surname index columns wherever a place has been so indexed. If these two columns are blank then no street or surname index has been compiled for that place. In this instance you simply proceed to the class list.

PLACE NAME	COUNTY ABBREV	DISTRICT NAME	DIST NO.	SUB D.No	STREET INDEX	NAME INDEX
Bentley	Hants	Alton	114	2		
Bentley	Staffs	Walsall	380	1		
Bentley	Suff	Samford	221	2		
Bentley	Warw	Atherstone	397	4		
Bentley	Yorks ER	Beverley	518	2		
Bentley	Yorks WR	Doncaster	510	4		
Bentley Pauncefoot	Worcs	Bromsgrove	392	3		
Bentley, Great	Essex	Tendring	203	1		
Bentley, Little	Essex	Tendring	203	5		
Bentley, Lower	Worcs	Bromsgrove	392	3		
Bentley, Upper	Worcs	Bromsgrove	392	3		
Bentworth	Hants	Alton	114	1		
Benwell	Northumb	Newcastle upon Tyne	552	1	552	
Benwick	Cambs	North Witchford	191	1		
Beoley	Worcs	Kings Norton	393	1	393	
Bepton	Sussex	Midhurst	93	2		
Berden	Essex	Bishop Stortford	139	2		
Bere Regis	Dors	Wareham	273	4		
Bere Regis	Dors	Blandford	270	1		
Berechurch	Essex	Colchester	204	1		
Bergholt, East	Suff	Samford	221	1		
Bergholt, West	Essex	Lexden	205	4		
Berkeley	Glos	Thornbury	327	1		
Berkeswell	Warw	Meriden	39|	|1861|	
Berkhampstead	Herts	Berkhampstead	14|			
Berkhampstead St Mary	Herts	Berkhampstead	14|			
Berkhampstead, Great	Herts	Berkhampstead	14|			
Berkhampstead, Little	Herts	Hertford	142	2		

PLACE NAME INDEX FOR 1861 CENSUS RETURNS

Robert M Ballantyne Literature (Chiefly Juvenile Fiction) RG 11/1357, f 9 p 11

2   CLASS LISTS

If you find there is no surname or street index for the place you wish to search, consult the place-name index and make a note of the registration district number in the column by the side of your place which is highlighted in yellow. You should next look at the class list for the appropriate year to find how places are grouped together and to ascertain the order in which you can expect to find them on the microfilm. The class list is arranged in numerical order of registration district so you need to discover the correct number before you look at the list.

In 1841 the census returns are grouped by hundreds, and in the northern counties, wapentakes, rather than by registration districts. From the place-name index you will be guided to the **page** of the class list where your place occurs.

In all other census years the place-name index will give you a registration district number. The class lists, arranged in numerical order of registration district, will show places grouped together by sub-district within each registration district.

Each civil parish will include townships and hamlets, not all of which will necessarily be found in the same sub-district or registration district. A cross-referencing system in the footnotes to the class list will tell you where the rest of the parish may be found.

Reference		HEREFORDSHIRE		HO 107
HO 107	HUNDRED	PARISH	TOWNSHIP	HAMLET
418	Broxash	Avenbury		
		Bodenham	Bodenham	
			Bowley	
			Bryan-Maund	
			Whitchurch-Maund	
			The Moor	
		Bredenbury		
		Bromyard	Brockhampton	
			(3)Linton	
			Norton	
			Winslow	
		Bockleton(part)*	Hampton-Charles	
		Collington		
		Little Cowarne		
		Much Cowarne		

			Llanveynoe	
			Longtown	
			Newton	
		Cusop		
		Cwmyoy(part)*	Bwlch Trewyn	
			Fwthog or Toothog	
			Llancillo	
		St Margaret's		
		Michael-Church-Eskley		
		Rowlstone		
		Walterstone		

HO 107/418	* Rest is in HO 107/1192	
HO 107/419	* Rest is in HO 107/1194	
HO 107/420	* Rest is in HO 107/742	1841

- 122 -

89221 Dd 104657 30m 10/78

When you discover the exact place you want, the number in the reference column of the list, together with the group and class code in the box at the head of that column, is the full reference you need to identify your film. See appendix 6 for a fuller explanation of the PRO referencing system.

Arthur Chappell   Music Publisher   HO 107/1475, f 410 p 20

Where a return does not survive the class list will show it as 'MISSING'.

Class lists also show you, by means of a bracketed number, the whereabouts of barracks, institutions and shipping. The key to these numbers is to be found in front of each class list and is as follows:

(1) barracks and military quarters
(2) HM ships at home
(3) workhouses (including pauper schools)
(4) hospitals (sick, convalescent, incurable)
(5) lunatic asylums (public and private)
(6) prisons
(7) certified reformatories and industrial schools
(8) merchant vessels
(9) schools

3 LONDON STREET INDEXES

If your search is in the returns for London you will certainly need a street index before you start to look in order to narrow your search. To attempt a search anywhere in London without such specific information is impractical; working through film after film on the off-chance of picking up one particular entry is a forlorn hope. The moment when you blink may be the moment the entry you want appears in the frame.

London is divided into about 36 registration districts, depending on the particular year (see appendix 7). After you have found in which registration district your particular street falls by consulting Book 90 (see 6 (i)), go next to the appropriate index in one of the London street index volumes on the shelves containing the finding aids for your particular census year. These follow the class lists on the shelves and contain the Western and Northern districts, the Central and Eastern districts and the Southern districts of London from Kensington to Greenwich. They do not include West Ham which, although considered part of London now, was in Essex in the nineteenth century.

STREET INDEX TO THE 1861 CENSUS

CLERKENWELL

Street		THE PIECE NUMBER OF YOUR FILM	TO FIND YOUR PLACE ON THE FILM
			Folios
Warner Street, Great, Great Bath Street	1-30	RG9/194	81-81
	pt 16	RG9/194	100
Warner Street, Little, Roy Street		RG9/191	78-82
Warren Cottages, Warren Street		RG9/195	100-101
Warren Street, White Conduit Street	1-33	RG9/195	93-105
	2B & 3½	RG9/195	100
	14	RG9/195	105
Warren Cottages		RG9/195	100-101
Waterloo Place, Clerkenwell Close		RG9/191	12-16
Wellington Place, Wellington Street		RG9/196	23-24
Wellington Street, Rodney Street	1-39	RG9/196	15-23
	Pt 5 & 13	RG9/196	36
West Place, Chapel Street	2-7	RG9/195	50-51
Weston Street, Pentonville Road	1-26	RG9/196	135-141
	1a & 1b	RG9/196	141
Wharton Street, Bagnigge Wells Road	1-35	RG9/192	66-73
Whisken Street, St John Street Road	36-62	RG9/199	77-90
White Conduit Place, White Conduit Street		RG9/195	82-83
White Conduit Street, Chapel Street		RG9/195	83-87
White Lion Buildings, White Lion Street		RG9/195	28-29
White Lion Street, Islington High Street			
	1-pt 46	RG9/195	1-9
	Penitentiary	RG9/195	33-34
	55-105	RG9/195	33-43
(Part 46 and 47-54 MISSING FROM			FD 1)
Wilderness Row, Gos			
Wilderness Row East			

1861 LONDON STREET INDEX

Each street index has a title page showing you the sub-district divisions and giving the piece numbers which cover those sub-districts. The index itself lists the streets, buildings,

1871 CENSUS			
STREET INDEX			
REGISTRATION DISTRICT 12			
H O L B O R N			
Sub-Districts	1	St. George the Martyr	RG10/369-372
	2	St. Andrew Eastern	RG10/373-375
	3	Saffron Hill	RG10/376-378
	4	St. James Clerkenwell	RG10/379-383
	5	Amwell	RG10/384-387
	6	Pentonville	RG10/388-391
	7	Goswell Street	RG10/392-395

terraces and areas together with house numbers. Each entry is followed by two columns of figures. The first is headed 'To Order Your Film' (or 'To Select Your Film' or 'The Piece Number of Your Film') and provides the reference of the film you require. The second column is headed 'To Find Your Place on the Film' and gives you a folio number, or set of folio numbers, where a particular street will appear on the film. All documents are foliated before being filmed as a security measure to ensure that nothing is omitted from the filming and to provide a reference number when you need to refer to a particular page. These numbers are stamped on the top right-hand corner of every other page of the document, the page without a folio number being identified as the reverse of the preceding page and taking the same folio number. For 1881 and 1891 this column will only show an enumerator's district number until the street indexes are standardised to show folio numbers instead. In due course this differential will not exist.

You may not necessarily find a street all in one place on the film. The enumerator liked to save his shoe leather, and whilst going up and down a street would also take in side streets where

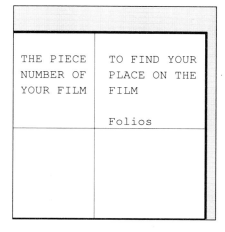

THE PIECE NUMBER OF YOUR FILM	TO FIND YOUR PLACE ON THE FILM
	Folios

they occurred, before returning to the main street to continue his rounds. You may, therefore, often find more than one sequence of folio numbers beside a street name, and also streets which are continued in other registration districts where boundaries cut across a road. This is explained more fully below in 'Finding Your Place on the Film' (p 31).

HM Alexandria Victoria The Queen HO 107/1478, f 645 p 19

In 1841 there is one slight difference in the referencing system. You will need a book number as well as a folio number to identify the whereabouts of your street. The foliation  in that year started again at the beginning of each book in the box, so that if you cite an 1841 reference without its book number but using a folio number only, it could mean one of several folios with the same number but in different books. The book number together with the folio number identifies a specific page. The book number can be found on every frame of the film as part of the reference strip and on the title page of each book (where the foliation begins at 1). There it looks like a fraction, the upper number being the piece number and the lower the number of the book.

4 COUNTRY STREET INDEXES

The country street indexes are much the same as the indexes to London registration districts. Places with a population of over 40,000 in the nineteenth century were street indexed. For a list of indexes available see appendixes 8-12. Most have a separate list of public houses, institutions and shipping at the back. Individually named buildings, terraces and groups of cottages are included, and each index has a title page showing the name of the registration district and its division into sub-districts. Country street indexes do not, however, show house numbers.

Hamlets included in any township are mentioned as entries in the index itself and not usually on the title page. Over the years other places with a population of less than 40,000 have acquired a street index, or a partial street index where not all of the registration district has been covered. These are not part of the normal run of indexes and will be found in a single volume, covering the years 1841 to 1871, on the officer's desk. They are listed in appendix 12.

Charles Landseer Historical Painter RG 9/56, f 124 p 36

STREET INDEX TO THE 1861 CENSUS		
CROYDON	TO ORDER YOUR FILM	TO FIND YOUR PLACE ON THE FILM
Street		Folios
Croydon Lodge, St James Road	RG9/450	31
Croydon Road	RG9/451	118–121
Crystal Palace Lodge	RG9/451	142
Crystal Palace Road, Norwood	RG9/450	78–79
Crystal Terrace	RG9/451	7–10
Dagnall Park	RG9/450	166–168
Dale House, Beaulah Hill	RG9/451	42
Dalletts Cottages, Merton Rush	RG9/453	89–90
Daltons Court, Church Street	RG9/449	71–72
Daniels Cottages, Whitehorse Road	RG9/450	48–49
Dartmill Cottage, New Town	Country Street Index	
Deerfield, Beaulah Hill		

5 SURNAME INDEXES

The PRO does not itself compile surname indexes. There are, however, numerous surname indexes produced by family history societies and published in booklet form, although many are now produced on microfiche instead. For the whereabouts of microfiche readers see the plan of the reference rooms in appendix 4. Most societies begin with the 1851 census but many have progressed to the other years.

Many of these surname indexes are available in the Census Room and more are added each week. If you wish to discover if a place has a surname index, make a note of the registration district number (there is a complete list of registration district names and numbers in appendix 7). Next, go to the drawers where the surname indexes are housed (see plan in appendix 4); you will find the indexes available arranged in numerical order of registration district in colour-coded envelopes. If no envelope is there for your registration district in the year you wish to search this means that as yet none has been donated. If a name you want is listed it should also show the reference of the film you need and a folio number which will help you to find your place on the film. See pp 31-42 for an explanation of how to locate places by the use of folio numbers.

John Sanger 'Equestrian Troupe' Circus Proprietor RG 9/2943, f 114 p 6

6 ADDITIONAL FINDING AIDS

6 (i) An index to London streets (Book 90)

When looking up an address in any of the London censuses it is essential to be sure of its registration district.   In some census years there are as many as thirty-six registration districts in central London, and you can waste many hours seeking a street in the wrong district 'unless you do some homework first.   It is not enough to consult a map, for it will not tell you the boundaries of a registration district in relation to the street names, and knowing that a street is in Marylebone today does not necessarily mean that it fell within the boundaries of the Marylebone registration district.   It may have been borderline and, in census terms, it may have fallen within St Pancras or Hampstead.   There is one sure way of finding out.

In 1887 the Metropolitan Board of Works published *Names of Streets and Places within the Metropolitan Area.*   This is an instantly forgettable title so the book is referred to as 'Book 90', from its reading room shelf number.   It provides a complete list of London streets, terraces, buildings, roads, etc (except for those which changed their name or were abolished before 1855), with the name of the nearest main road in a central column and the name of the parish in which they lie in the right-hand column.   The parishes named in the right-hand column are in most cases the same as the names of the appropriate London registration district but occasionally the name of the sub-district.   In this case a quick check in the book giving London parishes and localities (see 6(x)2) will identify the covering registration district for the given sub-district.   Then you can proceed confidently to the correct street index for the year you want by consulting the place-name index,   obtaining from it the registration district number,   and going to the appropriate street index volume.

Name.	Postal District.	Locality.	Parish.	Year
Wharves (The)	. S.E.	River-side . .	. East Greenwich .	
Wharves .The)	. W.	Uxbridge-road .	. Hammersmith .	
Wharncliffe-street .	. E.	Bonner-street .	. Bethnal-green .	1860
Wharton-place	. E.	School-house-lane	. Ratcliff .	
Wharton-road .	. W.	Sinclair-gardens .	. Hammersmith .	
Wharton-street	. E.C.	King's-cross-road	. Clerkenwell .	
Whateley-road	. S.E.	Kent-house-road	. B	
Whateley-road	. S.E.	Lordship-lane .	. C	Book 90
Whatman-road	. S.E.	Brockley-road .	. Lewisham .	1887
Wheathill-road	. S.E.	Croydon-road .	. Penge . .	1887

John Bird Sumner   Archbishop of Canterbury   HO 107/1571, f 291 p 4

6 (ii)   An index to abolished London street names (Books 91 and 92)

Sometimes London streets cannot be found in street indexes even though a birth, marriage or death certificate of a similar date clearly states the address. This is because street names changed, renumbering took place, or new streets were built.   When an enumerator collected his information it was quite possible that people still referred to their address by a recently discontinued name, or that a renumbering of a street obscured the fact that, for example, 86 King's Road was once 2 Victoria Cottages. The cottages may still be there with their name on the brickwork, but each of the individual cottages has acquired a number that is part of the road it is on, in place of the number of its particular position in the terrace or group of cottages. Much renumbering of London streets in this way took place in the 1850s and 1860s.

The way round this problem is to look in 'Books 91 and 92' which rejoice in the title *London County Council List of Streets and Places Within the Administrative County of*

		499										Wha—W
Name of Street or Place.	Locality.	Postal District.	Parish, Hamlet Precinct, or Liberty.	Metropolitan Borough, or City.	County Electoral and Parliamentary Division.	Ordnance sheet 5 ft. to 1 mile.	Reference to Municipal Map.	Name approved.	Date of Order.	No. of Plan.	Names abolished.	Rema
Wharf road	.. Pancras road	.. N.W	St. Pancras	St. Pancras	.. E. St. Pancras	vii.—23 33	23—12					
Wharf road	.. Frogmore ,	.. S.W.	Wandsworth Borough	Wandsworth	.. Wandsworth	x.—38	12—34	..	21.v.89	4227	Haydon's cotts.	
Wharf side ..	.. Lea bridge	.. N.E.	Hackney	Hackney	.. S. Hackney	iii.—89	38— 5					
Wharfdale road	.. Caledonian road	.. N.	Islington	Islington	.. W. Islington	.. vii.—33 34	25—13	..	24.vii.68	789	Wharf road Gordon terrace Albert place Albert terrace St.Stephen's terr. Haverford terr.	
Wharfedale street	.. Coleherne road	.. S.W.	Kensington	Kensington	.. S. Kensington	x.— 8	12—26					
†Wharncliffe gardens	Grove road, St. John's Wood road and Cunningham pl.	N.W.	St. Marylebone	St. Marylebone	W. Marylebone	vi.—49 50	16—15					
Wharncliffe street ..	Hartley street	.. N.E.	Bethnal green	Bethnal green	.. N.E. Bethnal green	vii.—38	37—14	1860	4.xii.85	3585		
Wharton street	.. King's Cross road	.. E.C.	Clerkenwell	Finsbury	.. Cen. Finsbury	vii.—44	26—15					
Wharves, The	.. Amberley road ..	W.	Paddington	Paddington	.. N. Paddington	vi.—48 49	13—16'					
Wharves. The	.. North and South Wharf roads	W.	Paddington	Paddington	.. N. Paddington	vi.—59 60	16—17					
Whateley road	.. Lordship lane	.. S.E.	Camberwell	Camberwell	.. Dulwich	xi.—67	33—35				.ace .et	
Whatman road	.. Brockley rise	.. S.E.	Lewisham	Lewisham	.. Lewisham	xi.—89	38—37	1867				
Wheatlands road	.. Tooting Bec road	S.W.	Wandsworth Borough	Wandsworth	.. Wandsworth	xv.— 1	18—41	1906				
Wheatsheaf lane	.. South Lambeth road	S.W.	Lambeth	Lambeth	.. Kennington	.. xi.—23	24—28	.,	8.xii.82	2971	Vittoria place Vittoria cottages Vittoria terrace	

London shewing Localities, Postal Districts, Parishes, Metropolitan Boroughs, Electoral Divisions, Ordnance and Municipal Map References Together with the Alterations in Street Nomenclature and Numbering since 1856. The Public Record Office has the revised edition, compiled by the Superintendent Architect of the Council and published in 1912. It is in two volumes: 'Book 91' covering A to Lily and 'Book 92' covering Limasol to Z. You will see in many cases a 'date of order' in a column after the street name; this means that at that date an order went through for some adjustment in the street name. Some time after this date the change would have been put into effect. These volumes, however, like Book 90, do not include the names of streets abolished or changed before 1855.

Joseph Tussaud Artist RG 10/164, f 13 p 20

6 (iii) Shipping index (Book 95)

Shipping on rivers and within territorial waters was included in the census returns at the end of the districts where the ships lay but it was not until 1861 that shipping on the high seas and in foreign ports was enumerated and then only some of it. Returns from such ships are found in the special shipping schedules at the end of the returns from 1861 onwards. There is an index to the names of ships compiled from these schedules and also a set of microfiche which indexes all the people on board for 1861 only. Both of these finding aids may be obtained by asking at the officer's desk.

6 (iv)   List of ecclesiastical parishes (Book 94)

It frequently happens that a particular place required by a searcher is an ecclesiastical district and cannot be found in the list of places because the census was enumerated in civil parishes. Obviously the ecclesiastical district exists, but it is necessary to determine in which civil parish it rests. To do this consult the list of parishes. This is a four volume book, bound in black, that will tell you in most instances the name of the ecclesiastical parish in the left-hand column followed by the civil parish in the next column. There is also a column giving the poor law union, which is the same as the registration district. Armed with the name of the registration district and appropriate civil parish you can discover the reference by the normal procedure.

Once you have the film on the machine and you have turned on to the civil parish indicated you will see, if the enumerator has done his job correctly, that there is a box at the top of the page labelled 'ecclesiastical district' which should be completed and therefore contain the place name you originally sought. If it is not, turn back to the title page of that enumeration district where you may find mention of the ecclesiastical district and be reassured that it has been enumerated in that part of the film.

James Burn   Editor of the ABC Railway Guide   RG 10/1322, f 62 p 12

19.

Name of Ship	Whereabouts	Reference RG 9
BACCHUS	Bristol	4498
BACCHUS	Llanelly	4530
BADGER	North Sea	4450
BALBIC	Liverpool	4507
BALCLUTHA	A.S.	4438
BALFOUR	Dudgeon Light	4463
BALLARRAT	At Sea	4458
BALLARAT	Dieppe	4459

Book 95

ESSI|

188

	Parish or Place.	United with or included in	Division.	County.	Description.	Tax Survey.	Poor Law Union.	Collector of I. R.
1	**Essington** -	Essington, &c. -	Cuttlestone -	Stafford -	Tp.	STAFFORD -	Cannock -	Wolverhampton.
2	**Estacott** -	(Northoe P.) -	Braunton -	Devon -	Ham.	BARNSTAPLE -	Barnstaple -	Exeter.
3	**Eston** -	- - -	Langbaurgh East	Yorks -	Tp.	STOCKTON -	Middlesbrough -	Sunderland.
4	**Estyn** - -	Caergwrley, &c.	Mold -	Flint -	Ham.	CHESTER -	Hawarden -	Chester.
5	**Estynallon** -	Bodlith, &c. -	Cynlleth and Mochnant.	Denbigh -	Tp.	WREXHAM -	Oswestry Incorporation.	Chester.
6	**Etal** - -	(Ford P.) -	Glendale -	Northumb. -	—	ALNWICK -	Glendale -	Newcastle.
7	**Etchells** -	Northenden, &c. -	Stockport -	Cheshire -	L.T.P.	STOCKPORT -	Altrincham and Stockport.	Manchester.
8	**Etchells in Northern**	Etchells in Northern, &c.	Stockport -	Cheshire -	Par.	STOCKPORT -	- -	Stockport.
9	**Etchilhampton** -	Etchilhampton, &c.	Devizes -	Wilts -	L.T.P.	CHIPPENHAM -	Devizes -	Bath.
10	**Etchingham**	- - -	Hastings Rape (Battle).	Sussex Yorks	Par.	HASTINGS -	Ticehurst -	Canterbury.
11	Etherdwick **Etherley**	(Escomb Tp.) -	Darlington Ward	Durham -	Ham.	DARLINGTON -	Auckland -	Sunderland.
12	**Ethy** - -	St. Winnow Lostwithiel.	- -	Cornwall -	—	BODMIN -	- -	Plymouth.
13	**Ethirick** -	(St. Dominick P.)	East Middle -	Cornwall -	Ham.	LAUNCESTON -	Liskeard -	Plymouth.
14	**Eton** -	- - -	Stoke - -	Bucks -	Par. & L.B.	WINDSOR -	Eton -	Reading.
15	**Etton** -	- - -	Peterborough -	Northampton -	Par.	PETERBOROUGH -	Peterborough -	Lincoln.
16	**Etruria** -	(Shelton P.) -	Pirehill North -	Stafford -	—	STOKE-ON-TRENT	Stoke-on-Trent -	Derby.
17	**Etterby** -	Brunstock, &c. -	Eskdale Ward -	Cumberland -	L.T.P.	CARLISLE -	Carlisle -	Carlisle.
18	**Ettiley Heath** -	(Sandbach P.) -	Northwich -	Cheshire -	Ham.	CREWE -	Congleton -	Chester.
19	**Ettingshall** -	(Bilston P.) -	Seisdon -	Stafford -	Ham.	WOLVERHAMPTON	Wolverhampton	

Book 94

The Duchess of Orleans HO 107/1604, f 122 p 37

6 (v) Hamlet index (Book 93)

Hamlets are places too small to have their own parish church and are generally found buried in the footnotes of the population tables. The Public Record Office has compiled an index to all small places in the footnotes to the population tables of 1851-1881 which give the parish and the registration district in which they will be found on the film. These hamlets are, however, now also included in the class lists.

PLACE	INCLUDED WITH	COUNTY	REGISTRATION DISTRICT
	SUPPLEMENTARY INDEX OF CENSUS PLACE NAMES 1851-1881		
Law Lee	Winterborne-Whitchurch	Dors	Blandford
Lawley	Wellington	Salop	Wellington
Lawton	Kingsland	Heref	Leominster
Lawton and Little Sutton	Diddlebury	Salop	Ludlow
Laxerton	Buckland	Glos	Winchcomb
Laxey	Lonan	Isle of Man	Isle of Man
Laycock	Keighley	Yorks WR	Keighley
Laymore	Crewkerne	Som	Chard
Lazenby	Wilton	Yorks WR	Guisbrough
Lea	Pontesbury	Salop	Atcham
Leacroft	Cannock	Staffs	Penkridge
Leadbrook Major	Northop	Flints	Holywell
Leadbrook Minor	Northop	Flints	**Book 93**
Leadon	Bishops Frome	Heref	
Leadon with Haffield	Ledbury	Heref	

6 (vi) List of churches and chapels wherein marriages are solemnised according to the rites of the established church 1871 (Book 96)

As its rather lengthy title suggests, this volume is a list of churches and chapels, grouped alphabetically by the name of the registration district into which they fall. Its value is that, having located a family in the census returns, a searcher may need to continue the hunt for families in parish registers. After consulting 'Book 96' you will know which parish or nonconformist registers to consult. This list is part of an annual series from which the one for 1871 has been selected for use in the Census Room. You may find when seeking parish records in the area in an earlier period that not all the churches listed in 1871 will be in existence. The ecclesiastical census of 1851 (HO 129 held at the Public Record Office, Kew) surveys places of worship at that date.

William T Mitford Magistrate Deputy Lieutenant RG 11/140, f 79 pp 13-14

Do not forget that if ancestors do not seem to appear in appropriate parish registers, they may have been nonconformist. Many researchers disregard nonconformist records, many of which are held in the Public Record Office in the record classes RG 4 to RG 8, because they assume that the family have always been Anglicans. Nonconformity was very popular in the nineteenth century especially amongst some classes of people such as industrial workers, artisans and tradesmen, and your ancestors may have tried what was the current trend. All nonconformist registers are indexed on the International Genealogical Index, a copy of which is available in the Census Room (see D Shorney, *Sources for the History of Non-Conformity* Public Record Office Readers' Guide, forthcoming).

6 (vii) London street directories

The London street directories are not only useful for tracing individuals from their known trades or professions, but can also help when you are faced with multiple entries for a street in a street index. Where there are several references in a street index, and no indication as to which one contains the house number you want, turn to the street directory. Look up your street, find your house number and note the names of the two side streets (written in italics) nearest to your house number, and then go back to the street index. Look up the references to the side streets and select similar references from the selection given for your long street. Remember that some streets may run on into another registration district.

The Public Record Office makes available the street directories for the year following a census year in order to allow for the compilation and printing of information gathered in the actual census year. Even so, as is often the case today, these may have errors at the time of going to press; so, if persons are not listed in the directory under the address you expect, you may still find them there on the film.

6 (viii)   Maps

Instinctively one turns to a map when difficulties are encountered in locating a place, either while searching in the indexes or after finding a birthplace on the microfilms. Sometimes it is much quicker to turn to a gazetteer or one of the additional finding aids before going to a map because most maps do not relate to census divisions.

The Public Record Office makes available a book of parish maps, known as the Phillimore Atlas, arranged by county, published by the Institute of Heraldic and Genealogical Studies at Canterbury and available for purchase from them, from the Public Record Office shop and from the Society of Genealogists. This is useful when a parish does not include the family you are looking for and you need to cast your net wider and search the surrounding parishes.

There are also two sets of maps in the Public Record Office at Chancery Lane which give the boundaries of the registration districts, sub-districts and the civil parishes. One set, correct for the years 1851 to 1861, is not complete, as some of the maps do not survive. The other is a complete set for 1891 (for both sets see the class list for RG 18). Note your registration district number when using the 1891 set since that is the way the maps are arranged within the counties.

These maps are most useful when an individual large house or a tiny hamlet cannot be found in street indexes or other finding aids. Once the place is located on the map the parish containing it can be determined by noting the place name which has a pink line through it within the thin red boundary line. Then note the sub-district by observing the pink boundaries within which the place falls, and the large pink spot on the place which gives its name to the sub-district. Finally, note the green boundary lines and the green spot on the place which is the name of the registration district, and return to the lists and indexes for the year you wish to research.

These maps are large documents so they need to be consulted in the reading rooms upstairs, for which you will need a reader's ticket, obtainable from reception. To apply for a reader's ticket you need to bring some form of identification such as a passport, a driving licence or a banker's card with your signature on it.

Copies of these maps may be obtained from the microfilm version; ask at the reading room officer's desk in the Census Room. The films are not as clear as the originals because the colour has not been reproduced and the fine detail of the map is difficult to read on film.

Charles Mark (Karl Marx) Dr (philosophical author) HO 107/1510, f 260 p 11

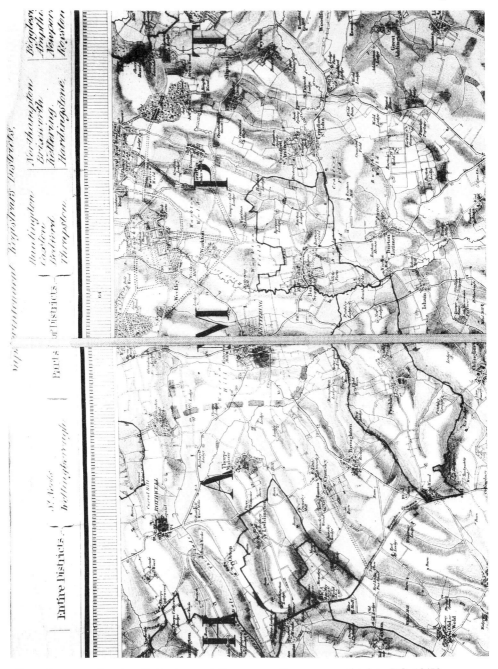

Part of a map showing Kettering and the surrounding census districts RG 18/52

The Greater London Record Office has published a list of known eighteenth-century maps of London; the Guildhall Library and the Bishopsgate Institute also have useful map collections. An *A-Z of Georgian London* and an *A-Z of Victorian London* have been published by the London Topographical Society; equally valuable is the series of Victorian Ordnance Survey Maps published by Godfrey.

The appropriate local record office or local history or family history societies may be able to help if you are in difficulties with any particular place. They will have local knowledge not available in the Census Room.

For the London area the Society of Genealogists has published a map showing London registration district boundaries in relation to borough boundaries and the boundaries of the local family history societies. This is available at the PRO shop and at the Society.

6 (ix) Population tables

Once the census returns had been thoroughly checked by the enumerators and their supervisors, the information collected was published as a set of Parliamentary Papers; copies of these for all census years may be seen at the officer's desk. The tables, like the class lists, are arranged in numerical order of registration district and give the breakdown of an area into registration districts, sub-districts and townships. They also give the acreage of each township. Then follows a count of houses and population for each place, both for

the year being enumerated and for the previous census year. The footnotes give useful additional information; eg why a local population varied markedly from the previous

610 YORKSHIRE—35. WEST RIDING.—Area ; Houses and Inhabitants, 1851				HOUSES.			
		Area in Statute Acres.		1851.			1
SUPERINTENDENT REGISTRAR'S DISTRICT.							
SUB-DISTRICT.	Parish, Township, or Place.		Inha-bited.	Un-inha-bited.	Build-ing.	Inha-bited.	
495. TODMORDEN.							
1. HEBDEN BRIDGE	*Halifax, part of* Parish—ᵃ						
	Wadsworth - - Township	10080	957	166	–	923	
	Erringden - - Township	2980	383	47	1	371	
	Heptonstall - ᵃᵃ Township	5320	882	127	2	790	
	Stansfield, *part of* ᵃ -ᵃᵃ Township [viz., the Lower Third Division.]		353	95	3	320	
2. TODMORDEN	*Halifax, part of* Parish—ᵃ	}5920{					
	Stansfield, *part of* ᵃ - Township [viz., the Middle Third and Upper Third Division.]		1132	102	11	1351	
	Langfield - - - Township	2620	752	41	55	890	
	Rochdale, part of Parish—ᵇ						
	TODMORDEN and Walsden } Townp. (*Lancashire*) - -}	–	1481	114	31	1790	
496. SADDLEWORTH.							
1. DELPH ᵇᵇ - -	Saddleworth, *part of* † - Township } (*part of Rochdale* Parish.ᵇ) }	}18280{	1819	230	10	2048	
2. UPPER MILL ᵇᵇ -	Saddleworth, *part of* (W) † Township } (*part of Rochdale* Parish.ᵇ) }		1548	105	18	1770	
497. HUDDERSFIELD.							
1. SLAITHWAITE -	*Huddersfield, part of* Parish--ᶜ						
	Slaithwaite - - Township	2320	553	29	7	575	
	Marsden { in *Huddersfield* Parish ᶜ	2050	103	9	6	138	
	Tnp.ᶜ ᵈ { in *Almondbury* Parish § ᵉ -	5061	407	50	4	428	
	Almondbury, part of Parish—§ ᵉ						
	Lingards - - - Township	500	159	4	–	149	
	Linthwaite, *part of* ∥ - ᶠ Township	809	264	13	–	309	
2. MELTHAM -	*Almondbury, part of* Parish—§ ᵉ						
	South Crosland Township	1360	536	36	2	582	
	Meltham - - Township	4525	684	42	20	795	
3. HONLEY - -	*Almondbury, part of* Parish—§ ᵉ						
	Honley (W) - .; ᵍ Township	2790	1077	35	17	987	
	Netherthong - - Township	850	223	13	5	223	

John W Millais Proprietor of Houses HO 107/1509, f 75 p 14

census, or where institutions (as defined on p 37), or lists of railway navvies, may be found. Copies of these tables are kept in the Census Room in case clarification is required of places falling within a registration district or information is needed about the fluctuation of population in an area. A list of these publications will be found in the bibliography (appendix 13).

6(x) Miscellaneous topographical indexes

As indexing of census returns has progressed over the years much useful information has been collected to assist in identifying the whereabouts of places and particular addresses, especially in London.

There are six indexes available at the officer's desk which may help to identify places which do not occur in the place-name indexes, or which may be useful when searching for places in London.

1. County variations and divided parishes
2. Parishes and localities
3. Divided streets
4. Renumbered streets
5. Missing streets
6. Postal districts

Identifying a particular part of London can be quite complex as some streets appear in more than one index. Ask the reading room officer to help you if you need to use these volumes.

Henry Ryman Manager - Stationery RG 11/195, f 4 p 1

FROM REFERENCE TO MICROFILM

Once you have discovered your reference then go and find your seat. Either side of the reference and photocopying rooms are several interconnecting reading rooms which house the microfilm readers and film cabinets (see appendix 5 for a plan of the reading rooms). Your seat number is on the edge of the table holding the microfilm reader and will be repeated on the black 'dummy' box located on a ledge to the right of each reader. Take this black box with you to the microfilm cabinets that you will find along one wall of most reading rooms (you may find your assigned seat is in a different room to that where your film is stored). The films are in numerical sequence of reference number and you will see that the cabinet drawers are clearly labelled with the first and last references held within them. When you open the drawer, you will find there is a locking mechanism which allows only one drawer in a stack to be opened at any one time. You will see the reference numbers marked on the side of the film boxes; select the one you need and replace it with the black box giving your seat number. When you return the film retrieve the black box. Please be sure to put your film back in the right drawer when you have finished with it. These film cabinets are locked at 4.30 pm every day, so if you finish

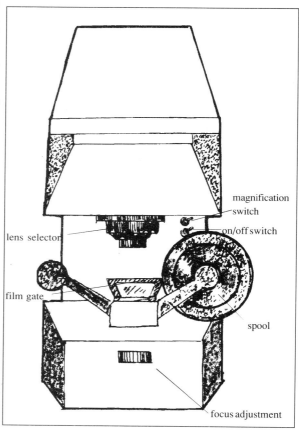

with a film after that time you cannot put it away. Just leave it on top of the cabinet in which it belongs and the staff will put it away and retrieve your dummy box later. Do not forget this cabinet locking time if you need to look at a film in the last half hour of the search room opening hours.

Alfred Tennyson   Poet Laureate   HO 107/1698, f 493 p 26

MICROFILM READERS

To thread your reel of film on to the micro-film reader you need to attach the reel to the spindle on the left-hand side of the machine. Next thread the film

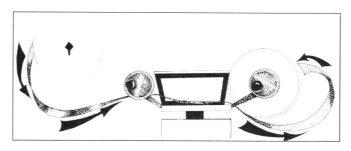

from the bottom of the reel to the right, under the gate and on to the empty spool on the right-hand spindle. Do not thread the film over the top of the right-hand reel but carry on moving the film to the right under the empty spool and bring it up on the outside of the spool and over the top in an anti-clockwise direction. Engage the end into the slot in the centre of the spool, as shown in the diagram. When going through the film quickly in order to reach a particular piece number, open the gate of the microfilm reader; there is then less wear and tear on the film. Once you are in the right piece number, close the gate and start looking at the detail.

You will find two lens settings directly above the gate which are changed by turning the bevelled wheel to the right or left as required. The on/off switch is to the right of the machine, and the focus button is in the front of the base. Microfilm readers must be switched off when not in use to avoid over-heating and damage to the film, which is liable to happen within even a few minutes. There are instructions at the reading room officer's desk, which explain how to load and operate a microfilm reader.

If the plastic spool is worn in the middle so that it will not run smoothly when turning the handle, ask a reading room officer to change it for you.

FINDING YOUR PLACE ON THE FILM

Once you have the film correctly threaded onto the machine you can start your search. Without having seen the original enumerators' books it must be difficult to understand the system you find. Remember that the enumerators handed out schedules to household-ers in the week preceding census night and collected them up on the Monday morning immediately after the Sunday night - it was always a Sunday - of the census (see appendix 1 for the dates of the 1841 to 1891 censuses). The enumerator then had to enter the information from these schedules into a book and provide a description of his district on

Edwin Landseer Artist HO 107/678, book 4 f 8 p 9

the title page. Some went further and provided maps or comments about the people they met. Most listed either the streets that were included in their enumeration district or the streets **surrounding** their area (in other words streets which do not appear in the following enumeration district but which define the area to be covered because they surround it). In 1891 the style of these title pages was altered to help clarify the parts of administrative divisions occurring in each enumeration district (see p 54). Even then it is difficult to discover exactly where some smaller places occur as the enumerators, having ·completed these new title pages, did not always repeat the place names in the box headings at the top of each page (see also p 65).The enumerator also had to complete a summary page of the totals of males and females and buildings he had encountered (see p 34).

Each of these books, therefore, has a title page, a page of instructions and a printed example of a completed form, a page of tables for the enumerator to complete, an abstract of totals and a page declaring that the information is correct (see pp 33-36). It is only after all this that the information about individuals begins.

The enumerators' books are bound into folders, about five or six at a time depending on their size. When these folders were filmed, they were first foliated for security, as a check that all had been included on the microfilm and to provide a precise reference when needing to identify a page. This means that the top right-hand corner of every other page is stamped with a sequence of numbers that begins and ends within that one folder, except in 1841 and 1851 when each box of folders was foliated throughout. Consequently when you obtain a reference for 1841 or 1851 it will cover more than a similar

reference for other census years. You will find that your piece number (the third element of your reference, see appendix 6) may cover more than one film, whereas for 1861-1891 you may get several piece numbers to a single film. So when you put your film onto the machine, depending on which year you are looking at, you need to make sure that you are in the right part of the film.

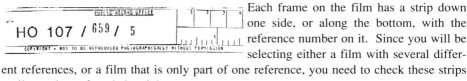

Each frame on the film has a strip down one side, or along the bottom, with the reference number on it. Since you will be selecting either a film with several different references, or a film that is only part of one reference, you need to check these strips until you have found the right reference for your place. Once you are into that part of the film you can narrow your search further.

William Hamley Toy Dealer RG 9/170, f 30 p 17

58

Superintendent Registrar's District _Portsmouth_

Registrar's Sub-District _Landport_

Enumeration District, No. _4_

Name of Enumerator, Mr. _Henry Dyer_

DESCRIPTION OF ENUMERATION DISTRICT.

[This description is to be written in by the Enumerator from the Copy supplied to him by the Registrar. Any explanatory notes or observations calculated to make the description clearer or more complete, may be added by the Enumerator].

From and including Lower Great Percy Street, both sides, along east side of Bagnigge Wells Road, including Police Court and Police Station. Along Kings Terrace North, taking Wharton Street North sides

Comprising

Nos 1st to 25th and 32 to 39 Lower Great Percy Street, Nos 27 and 28 Bagnigge Wells Road, Police Court and Police Station, Nos 1 to 8 Kings Terrace North, and Nos 1 to 15 Wharton Street North, Percy Grove.

Title page to an 1861 enumeration district   RG 9/192, f 58 p (i)

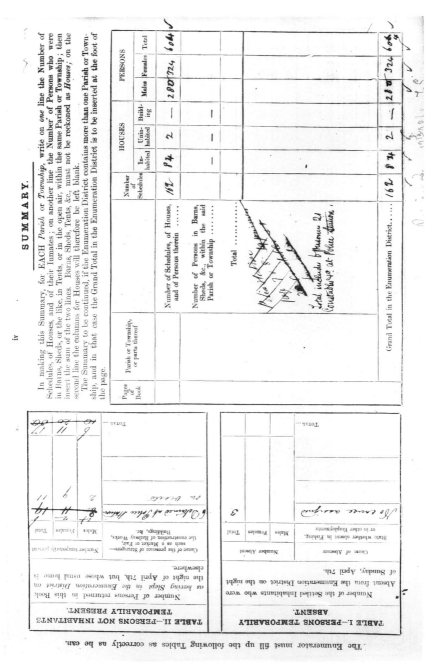

Summary page of an enumerator's book RG 9/192, f 59 p (iv)

ABSTRACT OF TOTALS IN THE FOLLOWING PAGES.

Page	No. of Schedules	Houses Inhabited	Uninhabited	Building	Males	Females	Total	Page
1	5	3			12	11	23	15
2	6	3			12	12	23	16
3	9	4			14	10	24	17
4	7	4			9	15	24	18
5	4	2			10	12	22	19
6	6	4	1		8	15	24	20
7	7	4			22	1	23	21
8	5	2			14	10	24	22
9	6	3			10	13	23	23
10	8	2			10	14	24	24
11	7	4			9	15	24	25
12	4	2			8	15	23	26
13	6	3			10	12	22	27
14	6	3			11	13	24	28
	80	40	1		159	167	326	

Continuation (right-hand half):

No. of Schedules	Houses Inhabited	Uninhabited	Building	Males	Females	Total	Page
5	3			10	16	26	29
5	4			12	13	25	30
6	3			9	14	23	31
7	3			11	12	23	32
6	3			12	10	28	33
6	3			9	12	21	34
10	5			12	12	24	
8	4			12	13	25	
6	6	1		8	16	24	
7	5			7	16	23	
8	3			13	11	24	
6				5	12	17	
82	44	1		120	137	277	

Note.—The number of Persons in Barns, Sheds, Tents, &c., must be entered against the page in which they occur, and the words "*Barns, Sheds, &c.*" as the case may be, must be written in the spaces for Houses.

RECAPITULATION.

Pages	No. of Schedules	Houses Inhabited	Uninhabited	Building	Males	Females	Total
1 to 14	80	40	1		159	167	326
15 to 26	82	44	1		120	157	277
29 to 31							
Total ...	162	84	2		279	324	603

Abstract of totals from an enumerator's book   RG 9/192, f 60 p (v)

vi

I SOLEMNLY declare that the Account of the Population and Houses of the District for which I am Enumerator, contained in this Book, has been truly and faithfully taken by me, and that, to the best of my knowledge and belief, the same is correct.

Witness my hand this *Fyfteenth* day of April, 1861,

Henry Dyer   Enumerator.

I CERTIFY that I have carefully examined the Account of the Population and Houses contained in this Book, and have satisfied myself by comparing it with the Householders' Schedules or otherwise, that the instructions have been punctually fulfilled and all defects supplied and inaccuracies corrected so as to make it as accurate as possible.

Witness my hand this 29½ day of *April* 1861,

W. Beauchamp   Registrar.

I CERTIFY that I have examined the Account of the Population contained in this Book, and that the Registrar has duly performed the duties required of him in regard to the same, and that no inaccuracies have been discovered therein which have not been duly corrected, as far as has been possible.

Witness my hand this 13½ day of *April May* 1861,

Wm Arthur Harbin   Superintendent Registrar.

Statement of accuracy from an enumerator's book   RG 9/192, f 60 p (vi)

Super-~tendent Registrar's District *Clerkenwell*	Enumeration District, No. *4*
Registrar's Sub-District *Amwell*	Name of Enumerator, Mr. *Henry Dyer*

DESCRIPTION OF ENUMERATION DISTRICT.

[This description is to be written in by the Enumerator from the Copy supplied to him by the Registrar. Any explanatory notes or observations calculated to **make the description clearer or** more complete, may be added by the Enumerator].

From and including Lower Great Percy Street, both sides, along . . . . Wells Road including . . . Police . . .

If you picked up a reference from the class list then you need to start looking at the title pages of the books which occur at regular intervals - remember there are five or six of these in each piece number - or at the boxed headings on each page for your place. Bearing in mind that each civil parish can contain numerous hamlets, tithings or townships, you need to search for your particular one before applying yourself to the information on the page.

If you have found your reference from a street index for 1841-1871 or a surname index, you will be seeking a particular folio number. Remember that a folio number covers two pages so do not just look at the page on which the folio number is stamped but also on the **following** page which, although without a stamped number, is the reverse of the page with the stamped number (see p 56). If your reference was

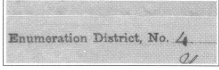

taken from a street index for 1881 or 1891 you will be looking for an enumeration district number which is written by the enumerator on the top right-hand corner of the title pages of the books on the film.

There are two exceptions to the above. Institutions such as workhouses, hospitals, asylums or military barracks, providing they contained at least two hundred inhabitants, were given the status of enumeration districts in their own right and are found at the end of each district on special forms which have no address column (see pp 38 and 39). The information given is sometimes not very useful as birthplaces are frequently not known ('N.K.'), but other records covering these particular categories may yield the information required. Similarly, shipping both in territorial waters and on inland waterways was recorded on special shipping schedules and these too are found at the end of the districts (see p 22). For an example of a completed shipping schedule see pp 40 and 41. Unfortunately not many of these shipping schedules survive in the 1891 returns.

Joseph Cash Mnf of Silk and Cotton RG 10/3182, ff 39- 40

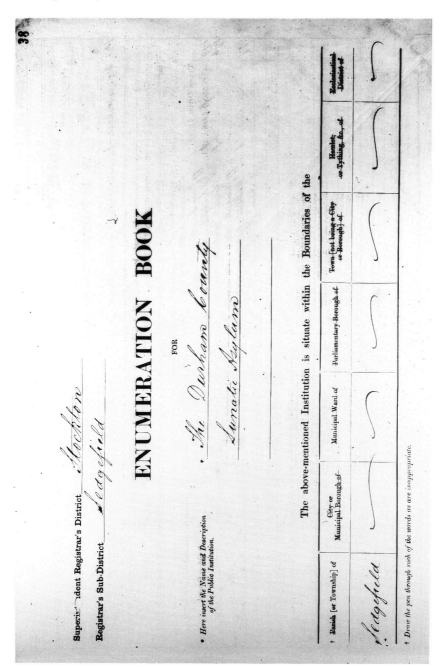

Title page to an institution RG 9/3696, f 38

NAME and SURNAME or Initials of Inmates	(1) RELATION to Head of Family—or (3) Position in the Institution	CONDITION	AGE [last Birthday] of MALES	FEMALES	RANK, PROFESSION, or OCCUPATION	WHERE BORN	If Deaf-and-Dumb or Blind
1	a.S. 215	Patient	Mar⁰		65	Pauper	o	
2	a.S. 6	do	Mar⁰		73	Washerwoman	o	
3	a.M. 7	do	Single		45	—	o	
4	a.L. 8	do	Do		57	Factory Hand	o	
5	H.H. 220	do	Mar⁰		39	Ladies Mk	o	
6	a.a. 1	do	Single		42	Womans Mfr	o	
7	H.G. 3	do	Do		45	Servant	o	
8	K.H. 4	do	Do		53	Dressmaker	o	
9	M.S. 5	do	Mar⁰	49	40	Servant	o	
10	L.H. 6	do	?		40	Joiner	o	
11	L.H. 9	do	Single	33		—	o	
12	R.E. 230	do	Do		46	Pitman	o	
13	M.J. 1	do	Do		45	Pauper	o	
14	M.B. 3	do	Do	54		None	o	
15	H.D. 4	do	Do	43		Mariner	o	
16	H.D. 5	do	Do			Joiner	o	
17	M.M. 6	do	Widow		36	Pauper	o	
18	M.J. 7	do	Single	64		Pelt	o	
19	J.D. 18	do	Do	41		Seaman	o	
20	M.E. 9	do	Widow		26	—	o	
21	M.C. 240	do	Mar⁰		61	Masons Wid	o	
22	P.M. 1	do	Do		42	—	o	
23	J.D. 2	do	Single	52		Soldier	o	
24	P.M. 3	do	Do	67		Labourer	o	
25	P.R. 4	do	Do	35		Mariner	o	
	Total of Males and Females				16			

Completed page showing institutional entries RG 9/3696, f 43

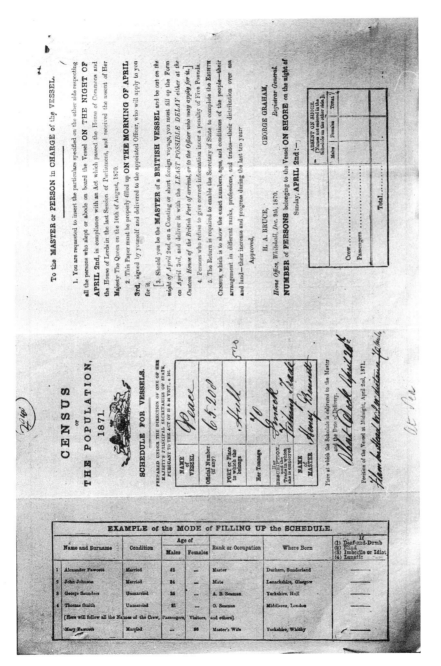

Shipping schedule for the fishing smack 'Peace' from Hull   RG 10/4797, f 134

134.

LIST of OFFICERS, CREW, and OTHERS on BOARD of the SHIP or VESSEL named the _Peace_ on the NIGHT of SUNDAY, APRIL 2nd, 1871.

	NAME and SURNAME	CONDITION	AGE (Last Birthday) Males	AGE Females	RANK or OCCUPATION	WHERE BORN	If (1) Deaf-and-Dumb (2) Blind (3) Imbecile or Idiot (4) Lunatic
1	Henry Bennett	Married	37		Captain	Ramsgate Kent	
2	Henry Scott	Unmarried	24		Mate	London Middlesex	
3	William Goulst		14		Fisherman	London Middlesex	
4	John Michael Mullet		14		Fisherman	London Middlesex	
5	Henry Galton		13		Boy	Hull Yorkshire	

I declare the foregoing to be a true Return, according to the best of my knowledge and belief.

Witness my Hand, Henry Bennett

Henry Bennett (Signature)

Completed schedule for 'Peace'   RG 10/4797, f 134

41

Remembering, therefore, that films for different years vary in their content, the following paragraphs explain each year's characteristics.

1841 Each film covers a series of small books. Each book has its own identifying number, marked on its first page. For example, piece HO 107/659 has books 659/1, 659/2 and so on. Each book has its own folio numbers on the top right-hand corner of every other page and may contain more than one enumeration district, the numbers of which are to be found on the title page of each district. This book number is also included on the identification slip which appears on the side or bottom of each frame of the film.

1851 Each piece has folio numbers which run right through the piece no matter how many separate books and enumeration districts are covered: they appear at the top right-hand corner of every other page. If a piece consists of more than one reel, the folio numbers covered by each reel are shown on the boxes. Wind on the film until you reach the folio numbers you were given in the reference books.

101

1861-1891 Each film covers a series of piece numbers which are foliated separately. Wind the film on to your piece number and look there for your place. If you have used a street index you can find your place by the folio numbers in the top right-hand corner of every other page, but for 1881 and 1891 turn to the enumerator's title page at the start of each district and look for your enumeration district number in the top right-hand corner.

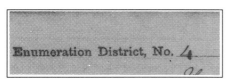

Then wind the film on and look for your street in that enumeration district.

Always make a careful note of reference numbers; it may be that you will need to refer to the same piece again in the future.

Charles Kean Tragedian HO 107/734, book 6 f 7 p 5

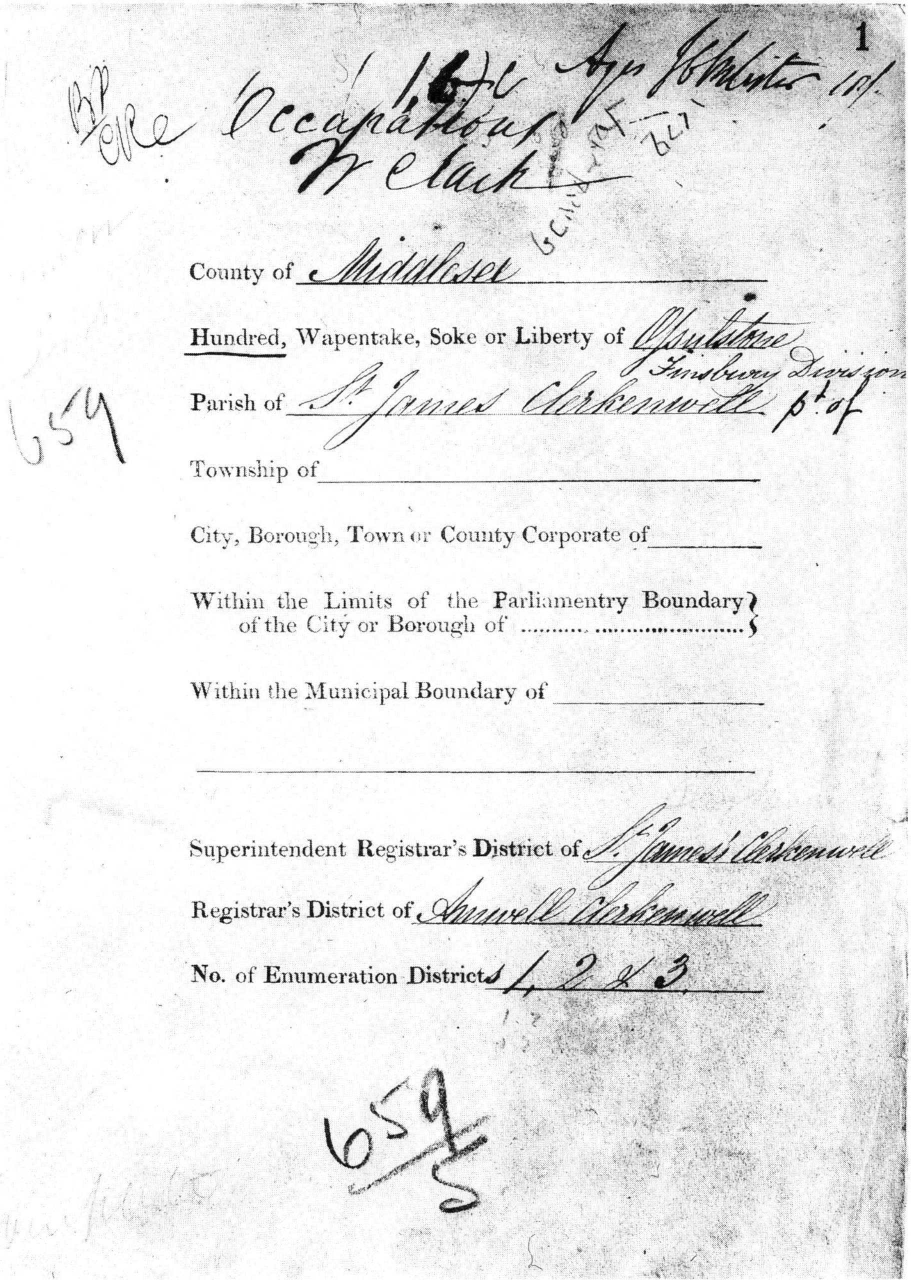

[handwritten form]

1

Occupations
W Clark

County of *Middlesex*

Hundred, Wapentake, Soke or Liberty of *Ossulstone*
Finsbury Division

Parish of *St James Clerkenwell p. of*

Township of

City, Borough, Town or County Corporate of

Within the Limits of the Parliamentry Boundary }
of the City or Borough of .... }

Within the Municipal Boundary of

Superintendent Registrar's District of *St James Clerkenwell*

Registrar's District of *Amwell Clerkenwell*

No. of Enumeration Districts *1, 2 & 3*

659

Title page of book 5 for 1841 St James Clerkenwell HO 107/659, book 5 f 1

UNDERSTANDING THE RETURNS

The information supplied for each individual recorded in the 1841 census returns is name and age (rounded down to the nearest five years for people over fifteen, though this instruction is not always followed), occupation, and some indication of the area of birth. Relationship to the head of household may often be assumed from the sequence of names and ages, although in 1841 this is not recorded. Divisions between families on the page are shown thus / and divisions between dwellings are shown thus //.

The letters in the 'where born' column have the following meanings:

Y - yes = born in county of current residence
N - no = not born in county of current residence,
    but born in England or Wales
I = born in Ireland
S = born in Scotland
F = born abroad

The 'occupation' column may have the following abbreviations:

NK - not known
FS - female servant
MS - male servant

The returns for 1851, 1861, 1871, 1881 and 1891 are more informative. In addition to the information supplied in the 1841 returns, they give the exact ages of the persons enumerated, their marital status, relationship to the head of the household, and exact place of birth. The column on the extreme right is the disability column which records whether the individual is 'deaf and dumb', 'blind', and from 1871, an 'imbecile' or 'idiot' or 'lunatic'. This final column was not completed as frequently as it should have been (see E J Higgs, *Making Sense of the Census* , p 75). In one instance an enumerator has used the expression 'idiot' for the person's occupation (RG 9/2139, f 64 p 23). From 1891 returns from Welsh registration districts, and those for Monmouthshire, recorded whether a person was Welsh or English speaking or could speak both languages. For a sample of completed census pages for the years 1841 to 1891 see pp 45, 47, 49, 51, 53 -55. The returns for 29 Wharton Street show the mobility of the Victorian population.

Benjamin Disraeli Privy Councillor RG 9/43, f 65 p 12

19

PLACE	HOUSES		NAMES of each Person who abode therein the preceding Night.	AGE and SEX		PROFESSION, TRADE, EMPLOYMENT, or of INDEPENDENT MEANS.	Where Born	
	Uninhabited or Building	Inhabited		Males	Females		Whether Born in same County	Whether Born in Scotland, Ireland, or Foreign Parts
Upper Wharton St			Emely D°		1 month		Y	
			Eliza Rowe		15	F S ✓	N	
29		1	William Capper	30		Linen Draper	Y	
			Jane D°		30		N	
			Edward D°	2			Y	
			John D°		5 months		Y	
			Mary Crundon		30	F S ✓	N	
			Wm Clive	15		F S ✓	N	
30		1	Eliz Kennedy		30	Ind	N	
Cumberland Cottage			Ellen Sullivan		25	F S ✓		I
		1	Wm Turnadge	50		Porter ✓	N	
			Martha D°		50		N	
Cumberland Place No 1			Charlotte D°		10		N	
		1	Clarke Tomalin	50		Clerk ✓	N	
			Isabella D°		35		Y	
			Henry D°	15			N	
			Mary Mahagan		20	F S ✓		I
2		1	Joseph Wilson	30		Merchant	N	
			Joseph D°	1			Y	
			Sarah Singer		20	F S ✓	N	
3		1	Charles Pitt	40		Ribbon Mfg	Y	
			William Connoly	25		S S ✓		I
4	J	1	Henry Duncton	55		Solicitor ✓	N	
			Rich D°	55		Accountant	N	
			Frederick D°	20		Printer	N	
TOTAL in Page 19				11	14			

29 Wharton Street inhabited by William Capper, Linen Draper, and family HO 107/659, book 5 f 40 p 19

Although the instructions issued to enumerators were very precise there are many instances where enumerators chose to stray from the rules and made observations or used unconventional terms to complete their returns. Title pages were intended to describe the district the enumerator had to cover but were also used by enumerators to add some comments of their own.

An enumerator in Beverley had carefully written out his instruction 'Enumerator must be careful and not take into the account any of the houses in St Nicholas Parish' and added 'Bow-Wow' (HO 107/2359, f 485). Others chose to voice their opinion on the neighbourhood they had been assigned: 'the houses marked marked thus x x x x in Close Alley are of a bad character consequently the information is doubtful the attention of the authorities has been directed towards them and several are closed' (RG 9/2455, f 67); and one lists the streets he covers with such remarks as 'all highly respectable, occupied chiefly by humble tradesmen, respectable shopkeepers' and so on (RG 9/5, f 90). One was so enthused with his district that he added 'I suppose a more laborious industrious and worthy community is not to be found within any other Enumerator's District' (RG 9/432, f 168). Another made the excuse 'this District being chiefly composed of the lower order of Irish such as an Lodging House Keepers, Pedlers, Rag Collectors, Chip Sellers, Bone Collectors, Hawkers of small wares, Beggers, etc. etc. I found it difficult to get at the proper description of some of the parties' (RG 9/2291, f 44). One concluded his summary with the poem:

'

So here you have the people all
From Brook Lane Farm to Puddingpoke Hall;
And here, in these mysterious pages,
You'll find the girls 'mysterious ages'.
The Sheep, the Wolves, in each vocation,
The Parson, Clerk & Congregation,
The Deaf, Dumb, Blind, the Wise, the Fools,
The Maids, Jades, Wives & Sunday Schools:
Publicans, Tailors, young Beginners,
Farmers & different sorts of Sinners.
Carpenters, wheelwrights & some Sawyers,
But free from Surgeons & from Lawyers!
Long life to all! and may the blushing maids
Next Census swell by splicing Brockford Blades!

(HO 107/1795, f 49 p iii)

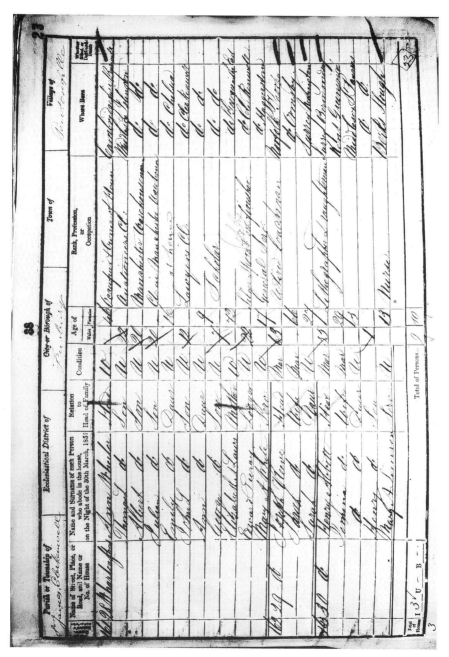

29 Wharton Street inhabited by Joseph Reeve, a retired coachman, and family
HO 107/1517, f 23 p 38

Other comments made by enumerators relate mainly to the difficulties of gathering the information, but in one case the enumerator felt he had made a mistake in entering the information of a Merchant Navy establishment into his book: 'please see further on for Officers of the Institution which I see should have been entered first. I am sorry that I have been so stupid' (RG 10/3775, f 95 p 5). The problems of gathering information were expressed by an enumerator in Brightside: 'to ensure accuracy in my district I after delivering the Schedules visited nearly every house a second time. In addition to this on the 1st of April I sent the Bellman through the district to request the Household to fill up their schedules and to supply anyone who might have been omitted during my visit. He says he could not find an omission' (RG 10/4693, f 55). Another difficulty encountered was by an enumerator who said 'the omission of the place of birth in the case of the Lunatics are too frequent; but I was utterly at a loss to make them out from their incoherency' (RG 9/647, f 87 p 39). In spite of efforts made to provide correct information, the census officer queried the total of houses enumerated in relation to those mentioned by the enumerator; there should have been 400 inhabited houses but the enumerator had only accounted for 288. The local supervisor, when challenged, replied: 'Having seen the Enumerator, Mr Thomas Lilley, he stated to me that the Memorandum Book is correct, as he did it himself, but employed a Junior Clerk to fill up the Enumerator Book which will have Caused discrepencies. Now I may say that Mr Lilley had this same District last time, and I thought he would have done it the best of any, I am very much grieved he has not' (RG 9/3841, f 86). In RG 10/4899, f 66 of Yarm, Stockton, the enumerator, William Thompson, has calculated that he walked 25 miles in the course of 'Distributing the sheddles (sic)' and collecting them up again.

Page 20

Parish [or Township] of St. James Clerkenwell

City or Municipal Borough of

Municipal Ward of

Parliamentary Borough of Finsbury

Town of

Hamlet or Tything, &c, of

Ecclesiastical District of St. Philips

The undermentioned Houses are situate within the Boundaries of the

No. of Schedule	Road, Street, &c, and No. or Name of House	HOUSES Inhabited	HOUSES Uninhabited (U.) or Building (B.)	Name and Surname of each Person	Relation to Head of Family	Condition	Age of Males	Age of Females	Rank, Profession, or Occupation	Where Born	Whether Blind, or Deaf-and-Dumb

Wharton Street

Total of Houses... 3 1

Total of Males and Females... 9 12

Eng.—Street D.

29 Wharton Street is uninhabited RG 9/192, f 70 p 20

Missing information: An enumerator in Manchester has explained the lack of information for one particular address by 'gross carelessness on the part of the Lodging Housekeeper. When I informed him to read the Schedule and told him of the penalty, it was all'to no purpose, he said he asked their names and they would not tell him' (RG 10/4051, f 160 p 51). In another case an enumerator has explained 'consequent upon a general Row when tables were turned over, three forms were destroyed and the names of thirty-seven persons, all males, of ages varying from 19 to 60, were lost ' (RG 11/322, f 35 p 16).

There is a note by a Superintendent Registrar: 'the foregoing sheets were filled up by the Reverend W J Palmer, the rector of Mixbury, but being incorect and Isaac Bayliss the Enumerator not being qualified for the Duty; W Thomas Hawkins of Brackley was apointed in his stead' (HO 107/886, book 12 f 13 p 21). Finally, there is evidence that one person was fined for refusing to give information: 'John Travers will not give any information respecting the persons who abode in his house on the night of June 6th only that the number was 125'. There is a note by the registrar that 'Mr Travers [was] fined £5 at the Mansion House by Sir Peter Lawrie June 23rd 1841' (HO 107/732, book 12 f 6 p 6).

29 Wharton Street inhabited by John Logan Grover, a solicitor, and his grandson. His housekeeper is not only a servant but is also the mother of his daughter-in-law! RG10/384, f 81 p 56

Doubts are often expressed that not everyone was included in the census and the remarks of one enumerator above prove this point. Efforts were made, however, to include even those people who had no address such as the three 'unknown men' recorded as 'heated by Japan stoves' in Aston in 1871 (RG 10/ 3138, f 106 p 37) and George Johnson of Barton-upon-Irwell 'living in an empty coke oven' (RG 9/2859, f 74 p 17). George Jones of Hereford, although usually living in Catherine Street, was recorded as a labourer 'in search of work walking all night'.

One condition, though normally married, unmarried, or widowed, was 'widow bewitched' (RG 10/4407, f 89 p 30). Also listed were a changeling (RG 10/ 4563, f 82 p 13) and an orphan 'stolen when a child by gypsies' (RG 9/432, f 12 p 18).

Addresses were not always a precise house number and street name. You can find a gin palace (HO 107/1495, f 565 p 56), someone living in a shed whose relationship to the head of the family is simply 'friendly' (RG 9/1783, f 35 p 22) and 'a factory for beds uninhabited at night' (HO 107/1500, f 389 p 48).

The clerks who analysed the information had instructions on how to categorise the many occupations but some recorded must have caused them to scratch their heads as no categories had been provided for them. Amongst the usual means of employment are listed a 'professional wizard' (RG 10/4684, f 30 p 6), two fugitive slaves (HO 107/2321, f 530 p 27), just 'aristocratic' with the comment in another hand 'Oh Dear' (HO 107/2171, f 224 p 19), a squatter from Queensland (RG 11/140, f 28 p 49), a nymph of the pavé (HO 107/1508, f 578 p 36), a runaway slave (RG 9/4127, f 83 p 14) and those that defied even those unorthodox descriptions, 'nondescript' (RG 10/1299, f 21 p 14) and 'generally useful' (HO 107/1528 , f 229 p 11).

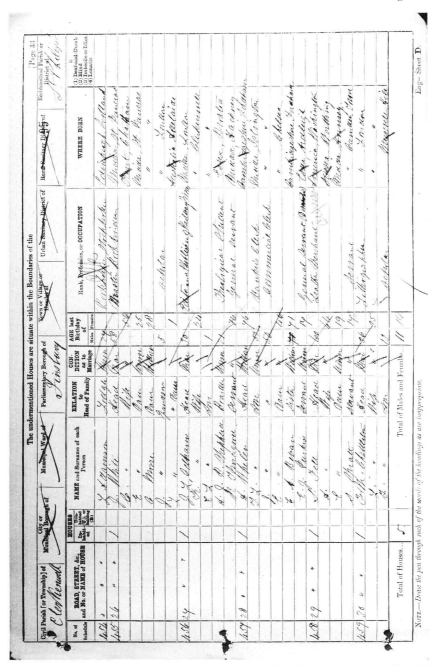

29 Wharton Street is now inhabited by S Fell, Leather Merchant, and family, John Logan Grover being now deceased RG 11/349, f 95 p 33

CENSUS OF ENGLAND AND WALES, 1891.

Registration District _Tunbridge_

Registration Sub-district _Tunbridge Wells_

Enumeration District, No. _1_

Name of Enumerator, Mrs. _Hannah Millie Hophoff_

DESCRIPTION OF ENUMERATION DISTRICT.

[The description of the District is to be written in by the Enumerator in Column 9 from the Copy supplied to him by the Registrar. Any explanatory notes or observations calculated to make the description clearer, or more complete, may be added by the Enumerator. It is especially necessary that the names of the various Local Sub-Divisions should be inserted in Columns 1 to 8.]

Cols.: 1	2	3	4	5	6	7	8	9
Civil Parish	Municipal Borough	Municipal Ward	Urban Sanitary District	Town or Village, or Hamlet	Rural Sanitary District	Parliamentary Borough or Division	Ecclesiastical Parish or District	Description of Boundaries and Contents of Enumeration District.

The Names of Local Sub-Divisions in Columns 1 to 8 should be written sideways.

RG 12/676, f 2 p i. A title page of an 1891 return for Tunbridge Wells showing the signature of a female enumerator. The following enumeration district was enumerated 54 by her brother and they themselves are enumerated on f 24.

29 Wharton Street has now been divided into two households RG 12/224, f 70 p 47

TO RETURN TO YOUR PLACE ON THE FILM

As you may need to refer to the entry again, you should note down the exact reference

while the film is on the reader. You will need the reference number that you used to select the film, the folio number and the page number. You will also find this referencing system essential to enable you to pass on specific information about your research to other census users.

Before the original returns were microfilmed folio numbers were stamped on the top right-hand corner of every other page. The rule is that a page without a folio number is the reverse of the preceding page and therefore has the same folio number when quoted for reference. To refer to a specific page of a folio you only need to give the folio number and state whether it is the recto (first side or right side) or the verso (reverse side) of the folio. Many people, however, prefer to use page numbers to identify which side of the folio they are referring to. If you use this method beware of the many sequences of page numbering used in the census. The page numbers are printed on each page and are preceded by the word 'page' except for 1841 and 1851 when they appear in the centre and at the top of each page.

If your search is in the 1841 census you will also need a book number, because each piece covers a series of small books which have their identifying number marked on the first page and are foliated separately. It can be found on the reference strip on the side or on the bottom of the frame.

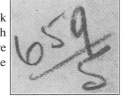

Having found what you want, make a note of the folio and page number and then roll back the film to the first folio of that sequence, where you will find folio '1', and look

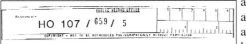

at the bottom of that page, which will have a figure like a fraction with the piece number above and the book number below. The book number is also noted on the reference strip on the side or the bottom of each frame of the film. Check that you have correctly recorded these two numbers.

William Gladstone MP HO 107/739, book 3 f 8 p 8

PHOTOCOPIES

If you would like a photocopy of part of the census returns, before removing the film from the microfilm reader you need to identify the frame of film you require (note that poor quality originals or scratched films will not reproduce high quality copies).

If you are unsure as to how to identify the correct frame, **leave the film on your reader, switch the reader off, and consult an officer.**

To obtain photocopies you need to know the full reference number including:

1841 - the book number and the folio number,
eg:
        HO 107/659, book 5, folio 3

1851-1891 - the folio number and the page number, eg:

        HO 107/1595 folio 243 page 29
        RG   9/1053   folio 136 page 1
        RG 10/653   folio 122 page 6
        RG 11/1253   folio 43   page 12
        RG 12/456   folio 29   page 16

See also appendix 6.

Postal applications for photocopies must have full correct references including folio numbers and page numbers.

There is one other factor you should consider if you plan to reproduce a document (ie to quote substantial parts of it or to print photographs or other copies of it). All census returns are subject to Crown copyright (see appendix 3).

George Du Maurier Artist 'Punch' RG 11/166, f 99 p 19

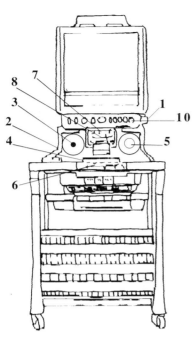

A4 Microfilm Photocopier

1 Turn power on.
2 Swing carriage towards you on the left.
3 Place film on left hand carriage spindle.
4 Feed film trailer under the first two rollers as far as possible, and press the blue button. Film will automatically feed onto the take up spool.
5 Advance film with the control knob. Only partially turn knob for slow advance.
6 Position image on screen by moving scanning lever as required.
7 Turn blue spiked wheel to adjust zoom.
8 Turn grey spiked wheel to adjust focus.
9 To make a copy place card in slot.
10 Press green print button.
11 Rewind film onto original spool.
12 Remove film and replace in box.
13 Switch unit off using power switch.

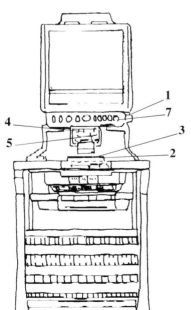

A4 Microfiche Photocopier

1 Turn power on.
2 Place film under glass.
3 Position image on screen by moving the carriage as required.
4 Turn blue spiked wheel to adjust zoom.
5 Turn grey spiked wheel to adjust focus.
6 To make a copy place card in slot.
7 Press green print button.
8 Switch unit off using power switch.

Place card in slot ◥

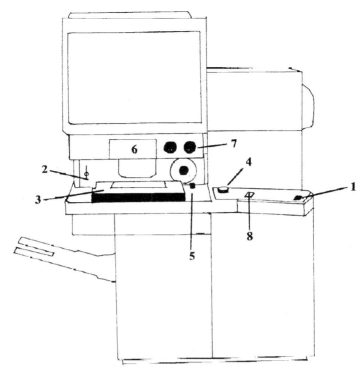

A3 Microfilm Photocopier

1 Press once to light screen.
2 Place film on left-hand carriage spindle.
3 Feed film trailer under the first two rollers as far as possible, and press the blue button.
  Film will automatically feed onto the take up spool.
4 Advance film with the control knob.
  Only partially turn knob for slow advance.
5 Position image on screen by moving scanning lever
      as required.
6 Zoom lens located behind door. Pull at left-hand to open.
  Adjust the image size by turning the top rubber grip.
7 Focus the image with focus control.

To make a copy

8 After placing card in slot, touch the green button.
4 Rewind film onto original spool.
2 Remove film and replace in box.
1 Press once to switch off screen.

PROBLEMS AND HOW TO SOLVE THEM

MISPLACING YOUR NOTEBOOK

It is a good idea to put your name and address in the front of your notebook. Nothing is more soul-destroying than to leave it somewhere knowing that you will not be revisiting that place for a few weeks. The Census Room staff will automatically return notebooks that have an address inside the cover.

FAILING TO RECORD REFERENCES

Another good practice that may not become apparent until you are well into your research is to **keep an exact reference** of every search you have done, even if it is unsuccessful. It will save hours of duplicate searching when a year or two later you are planning what to look at next and need to remember exactly what you have already examined. It will also be invaluable to relations researching other branches of your family (see appendix 6).

MISSING INFORMATION

Families

If families do not appear where expected there are various possible explanations.

There was some deliberate evasion of the enumerators. Turner, the painter, for instance, is reputed to have spent census night on a boat on the Thames to avoid being enumerated. Evasion was, however, more usually practised among the lowest ranks of society and especially by criminals.

Working class families appear to have moved from house to house with surprising frequency, and the address taken from a certificate may be out-of-date a few months later.

Many more people leased their houses than do now. This meant that they moved frequently when leases ran out. However, they most probably needed to be within easy walking distance of the same job. If you cannot find a family at a particular address look round the neighbourhood; they may not be far away.

Henry Irving Comedian RG 11/95, f 31 p 19

Charles Dickens is to be found staying with Robert Davey a medical practitioner at 34 Kepple Street, St George, Bloomsbury. He is listed as 'a visitor aged 39 author born Portsmouth, Hants' and with him, also visitors, are 'Alfred Samuel Dickens married 29 an engineer born Chatham, Kent and Augustus Newsham Dickens married 23 a merchants clerk born London'.

HO 107/1507, f 206 p 16

His family, but not his wife, are to be found at their home 1 Devonshire Terrace in Marylebone. Mary Dickens aged 12 is described in the column headed 'Relationship to Head of Household' as daughter of Charles Dickens and her occupation is again 'Daughter of Charles Dickens'. With her are listed Catherine, 11, Francis, 7, Alfred, 5, Sidney Smith, 4, Henry, 2, and Dora Ann 8 months, with a cook, wetnurse, and nurse.

HO 107/1488, f 207 p 9

Mrs Dickens is away from home and can be found staying in a Lodging House with her sister at Knotsford Lodge, Great Malvern whilst, presumably, taking the waters. The entry reads: 'Catherine Dickens lodger married 35 born Edinburgh and her sister Georgina Hogarth lodger unmarried 24 born Edinburgh'.

HO 107/2043, f 98 p 21

The people you are looking for might not have been at home on census night, in which case they will appear at the address where they were staying. In the 1851 census the Dickens family are a very good example of this.

Films

1. Folio numbers may be missing from the sequence: this means that the folio was missed when filming. In this case ask the officer if it is possible to see the original or, where this is not possible, to have the original checked for you.

2. If page numbers are missing from the sequence (but the foliation is correct) the folio did not survive. This situation most often occurs at the back or front of a book which has lost its covers. Unfortunately there is no solution. Another census year should be tried.

3. Some places are missing from the films: these are described as 'MISSING' in the class lists. There is no solution as the enumerators' books disappeared before the returns were transferred to the Public Record Office.

Items missing from indexes

Streets missing from the indexes suggest a number of possibilities:

the street had not yet been built;
the street was being built at the time;
the street was not yet named as such and the houses
  are identified by the name of villas, terraces, etc;
the street was missed by the indexers;
or the folio did not survive and so could not have been
  indexed.

If this happens in a London index look in Book 91 or 92 (see 6 (ii) p 21) to find the date of approval of the street name or the name of the villas, terraces, etc from which the street was formed. If this does not provide a satisfactory answer then try the street index for another year, and determine at least the sub-district into which it falls; otherwise find another street with the same reference as the street you seek. Then look up the same sub-district or other street in the year you are researching and check the film in case the individual houses or actual street appear in that part of the film and have been missed or disguised in the index.

Items missing from microfilms

1. Houses may be missing from streets: many streets were not numbered until long after they were built and were composed of named villas, terraces, cottages, buildings or individual houses which later remained under those names but were also numbered as part of the longer 'mother street'. Such houses may feature in the index under their former names.

2. Numbers are often missing from streets, since the numerical sequence of houses was erratic in the last century; on the other hand some streets had as many as four separate sequences of house numbers. At a later date this may have been rationalised, but it sometimes pays to continue looking through all references to a street in case the people you seek are indeed living at the house number you expect, but not at the particular house you are looking at because that has a duplicate number. In other words, there might be another

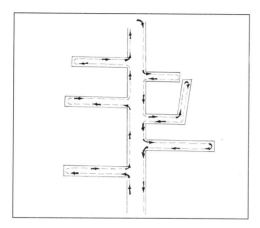

5 Hallam Street further on in the enumeration district. However, not all enumerators bothered to record house numbers and just entered the name of the road.

3. If house numbers are apparently missing from their sequence, this is because house numbers do not necessarily appear in sequence. The enumerator probably took the shortest route through his district. He may have begun at one end of a street (not necessarily number 1), walked down to the next crossroads, turned into a side street, then continued with the first street, ending up finally with number 1 when he reached the end of his rounds several crossroads later, on the other side of the street in which he started.

If only even, or only odd, numbers are recorded it probably indicates that the street was incomplete and only one side was built. It can also mean, however, that one side of the street was in one enumeration district and the other side of the street was in the next enumeration district, or even that the street was split between several enumeration districts where the boundaries

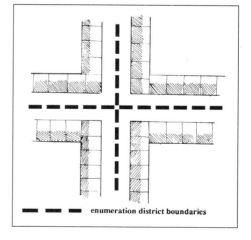

enumeration district boundaries

of an enumeration district occur at crossroads. The street index will cross refer you to other parts of the census where the rest of the street occurs.

Francis Reckitt Manufacturer of Starches, Blues, Black Lead, and of Machine and Fancy Biscuits by Steam RG 9/3592, f 75

In large towns, especially in the Midlands, you will find named buildings and courts listed in the street index. This is where an alleyway leading off a street opens into a courtyard round the sides of which are numerous dwellings, probably several storeys high.

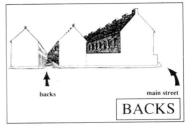

backs   main street

BACKS

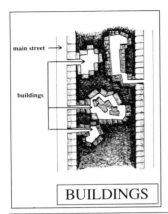

main street →

buildings

BUILDINGS

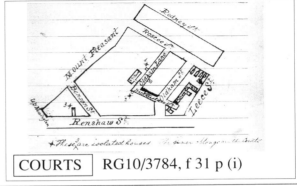

COURTS RG10/3784, f 31 p (i)

SUBJECT OF ENQUIRY IN OLDHAM REGISTRATION DISTRICT

Enumeration District 16

From Mr William Ascroft to Mr James L Page, enumerator

Please give a description of the premises designated "Cellar Dwellings" in the Memorandum Book of this District -

Whether they are Cellars <u>under Houses</u> or separate and distinct habitations called "<u>Cellar Dwellings</u>" -

Please return the Memorandum Book (5 September 1861)

Answer

In answer to your inquiry the term Cellar Dwellings applies to Dwellings under houses in cases where the Ground floor of the Houses are level with the front Street and the Floor of Cellars under the Ground floors are level with a Back Street. The Houses (so called) and the Cellar Dwellings (so called) being in the occupation of seperate tenants - I may somewhat elucidate the matter by saying that the Front Streets have been raised, after the original construction of the Streets and the erection of the Houses: <u>to avoid great declivities</u> and Render the ascent to various parts of the Town easier whilst the Section of the Surface of the Land at the Back has been left in its original State - Afterwards advantage has been taken of making seperate dwellings to face front and back. <u>No connexion existing between such seperate dwellings</u>.

RG 9/3010, f 51

4. If families are missing from houses, they may have been away from home on census night. The purpose of the census survey was to record not only individuals but also buildings, and thus the building in which they normally lived would have been recorded as 'uninhabited'.

If a house was uninhabited on census night it will still be enumerated but will probably be identifiable only by its place between two others. There is a column for uninhabited houses on the enumerator's form.

Missing places: Places missing from a class list means that a particular part of the census did not survive; another year should be tried. Places may be missing from a place-name index because the place being sought may be the name of an ecclesiastical parish instead of the civil parish on which the census was based. The List of Parishes (Book 94) should provide the answer (see 6 (iv) p 22). It lists most place names and in the second column on the page it will tell you in which civil parish they occur. Smaller places than a civil parish can be difficult to locate in the 1891 census. The newly designed title pages enabled the enumerator to break down his allotted patch into various administrative divisions, parts of which would be in his enumeration district and parts in other enumeration districts. Most can be ignored when searching the returns as the civil parish is the most useful unit for identifying a place in census terms. However, it is very often a township, village or hamlet within this civil parish that one needs to identify. At first glance this breakdown of places on the title page makes this identification easier. However, when you turn to the pages which follow, the box headings are frequently, but luckily not always, ignored by the enumerator which means that location of a particular hamlet or township is impossible unless you happen to know the names of the streets in that hamlet.

HOUSES	
In-habited	Unin-habited
1	
	2U
1	

Birthplaces: As far as the place of birth entry is concerned, you should remember that many people did not know where they were born, and some others lied about it, fearing that the information might be used to send them back to their home parish, as the Poor Law directed.

Some enumerators, being local men, would not know the place names of the part of the country whence the person they interviewed came. This, combined with a 'foreign' local accent, might produce a place-name spelling that will not occur in any gazetteer or map. If this happens try pronouncing the name given as a local might have done. Perhaps the 'H' has been missed at the beginning.

Ages: Ages given in the returns are not always reliable; some people did not know exactly when they were born and there were many reasons for lying about one's age.

HOW TO INDEX THE RETURNS

At first sight there is a bewildering variety of census indexes; but they fall into clearly defined categories as already noted (see 'Using the Reference Room' above). The first place to look is in the place-name index for your particular census year, or go to a street index if this is more appropriate. Copies of these indexes are provided by the PRO.

However, family history societies have, for the past decade, been busy compiling another type of index. Different researchers need different pieces of information, and family historians need names before they need places. Transcripts are never really necessary unless the document is not to be made available because it is fragile; researchers should always check an original source rather than rely on someone else's translation or interpretation, which can, even with the best intentions, go astray. It is far more sensible, therefore, to compile an index only. The recommended minimum content for a census index is surname, forename, age, birthplace and reference. If some uniformity is applied to census indexing it will be possible in the future to combine local indexes into a national one, which will be far easier to use. The Public Record Office has several surname indexes that have most generously been donated by family history societies, and more would be appreciated.

Anyone planning to index census returns for publication should adopt the method of referencing used in the Census Room. Then, anyone quoting a reference or placing an order for a photocopy at the Public Record Office, or asking for help in deciphering entries, would be talking the same 'language'. Searchers are frequently asked by the Census Room staff to return to their local record office or library and look again at the film to find the reference required since the information given is insufficient to locate the precise entry at the PRO. All this is time wasting. Individual methods of indexing, while appropriate in the smaller context of a local record office or library, are inadequate when applied to the holdings in the PRO, and it is vital that the complete PRO reference, including the folio and page number, is quoted, though you may find it easier to use the archival terms recto and verso instead of a page number (see also page 56 for folio numbers and page 57 for examples of complete references). All the original enumerators' books are foliated before being microfilmed, which means that one can go straight to the page required, but frequently the folio numbers are disregarded by indexers (see page 56).

Another important factor to consider when planning a census project is the area covered by the index. The census has its own in-built natural divisions for ease of enumeration. It is sensible, therefore, to use these divisions when defining the size of the index. The easiest unit to use, from a searcher's point of view, is that of the registration district. If this is too large to manage then an index to a sub-district is a suitable alternative. Both of these units will be more than one piece number (the archival term for an individual item and the third element of your reference number)

Byron Family Baron Byron BA RG 11/95, f 29 p 15

and some people do index one piece number only. This can be confusing to a user of the index because it is not easy to define just one piece as being part of a whole. Worse still, some indexers choose a parish as a unit for indexing. Not only does this sometimes mean that you need to index part of a piece number, but also many searchers are unaware of the fact that census parishes are civil ones and 'parish' in its usual form refers to an ecclesiastical district. The question arises, 'which type of parish is being indexed?' When providing an index, therefore, to a particular set of documents it is much more user-friendly to remain within the natural framework of the documents themselves.

1881 CENSUS PROJECT

The British Genealogical Record Users Committee (an informal group with representatives from the Federation of Family History Societies, the Society of Genealogists, the Institute of Genealogical and Heraldic Studies, the Public Record Office, and the Genealogical Society of Utah among others) have made the 1881 census the object of a national indexing project.

To avoid duplication of effort because so much work had already been done on the 1851 census, it was decided to concentrate on the 1881 census for England and Wales. The thirty-year gap in time between the two will help a new generation of researchers for whom the 1881 census will provide essential information at the beginning of their work.

The Genealogical Society of Utah (GSU), with permission from HMSO, will lend microfilm or photocopies of the 1881 returns to volunteers wishing to participate in the project. They will also provide forms onto which these may be transcribed, and after checking, the completed transcriptions will be collected and transferred to a computer data base by the GSU, or other volunteers.

The resulting data will then be made available on microfiche, both as a full transcript of the returns and as an index to them. Initially the index will be arranged by county and then by surname and given name: a format easily recognisable to those who have used the IGI. Other arrangements will also be possible and no other census will be so easily accessible. Anyone is welcome to join in and create a very important finding aid to the most popular record in the world.

If you require further details, send a stamped addressed envelope to the National Co-ordinator: Mr Richard Sowter, 2 Hill House Road, Downend, Bristol BS16 5RR.

76.

Page			The undermentioned Houses are situate within the Boundaries of the							
*Civil Parish [or Township] of *Isleworth*	City or Municipal Borough of	Municipal Ward of	Parliamentary Borough of	Town of *Hounslow*	Village or Hamlet, &c., of	Local Board, or [Improvement Commissioners District] of	Ecclesiastical District of *Holy Trinity*			

No. of Schedule	ROAD, STREET, &c., and No. or NAME of HOUSE	HOUSES In-habited / Un-inhabited / Building	NAME and Surname of each Person	RELATION to Head of Family	CON-DITION	AGE of Males / Females	Rank, Profession, or OCCUPATION	WHERE BORN	1 Deaf-and-Dumb 2 Blind 3 Imbecile or Idiot 4 Lunatic
	Tent		Not known						

FINIS

The first and last of W. Allott, taking the Census of England & Wales under the price gone up.

Alpha & Omega

Total of Houses..			Total of Males and Females..			2 / 5			

* Draw the pen through such of the words as are inappropriate.

RG 10/1313, f 43 p 44   Not all enumerators were happy in their work!

68

APPENDIX 1   DATES AND POPULATION

The dates for the taking of the census are as follows:

1841	June 6	Population of 15,914,000
1851	March 30	Population of 17,928,000
1861	April 7	Population of 20,066,000
1871	April 2	Population of 22,723,000
1881	April 3	Population of 25,974,000
1891	April 5	Population of 28,999,725

APPENDIX 2   CENSUS DIVISIONS

1   London within LCC boundaries;   see map opposite

2   South Eastern - Surrey and Kent (extra-metropolitan),
        Sussex, Hampshire, Berkshire

3   South Midland - Middlesex (extra-metropolitan),
        Hertfordshire, Buckinghamshire, Oxfordshire, Northamptonshire,
        Huntingdonshire, Bedfordshire, Cambridgeshire

4   Eastern - Essex, Suffolk, Norfolk

5   South Western - Wiltshire, Dorset, Devon, Cornwall and
        Somerset

6   West Midland - Gloucestershire, Herefordshire, Shropshire,
        Staffordshire, Worcestershire, Warwickshire

7   North Midland - Leicestershire, Rutland,
        Lincolnshire, Nottinghamshire, Derbyshire

8   North Western - Cheshire, Lancashire

9   Yorkshire

10   Northern - County Durham, Northumberland,
    ,   Cumberland, Westmorland

11   Welsh - Monmouthshire and
        Wales

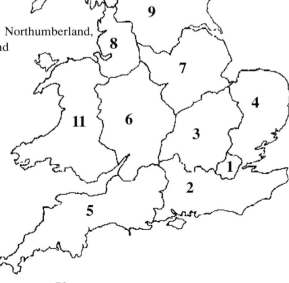

Division 1

1	Kensington	19	London City
2	Chelsea	20	Shoreditch
3	St George Hanover Square	21	Bethnal Green
4	Westminster	22	Whitechapel
5	St Martin in the Fields	23	St George in the East
6	St James Westminster	24	Stepney
7	Marylebone	25	Poplar
8	Hampstead	26	St Saviour Southwark
9	Pancras	27	St Olave Southwark
10	Islington	28	Bermondsey
11	Hackney	29	St George Southwark
12	St Giles	30	Newington
13	Strand	31	Lambeth
14	Holborn	32	Wandsworth
15	Clerkenwell	33	Camberwell
16	St Luke	34	Rotherhithe
17	East London	35	Greenwich
18	West London	36	Lewisham

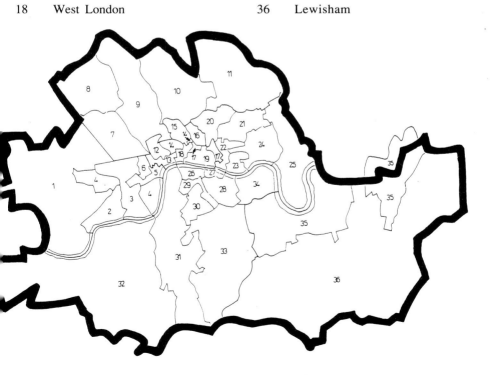

APPENDIX 3   COPYRIGHT IN CENSUS RETURNS

All British census returns are Crown copyright.   Unauthorised reproduction of the returns - whether in facsimile or transcript - may infringe copyright.

1. Making copies from microfilms

The Public Record Office has no objection to the reproduction of limited quantities of hard copy print from microfilms of the census returns held by local libraries, family history societies, and other non-profit-making organisations.   It is perfectly acceptable for holders of such microfilms to supply, for example:

a)   single copies of isolated pages to individuals for purposes of research or private study;

b)   single copies of consecutive pages covering an area of one complete parish, to local or family history societies or individuals, for purposes of academic or other non-commercial research including the compilation of indexes to the returns;

c)   multiple copies of isolated or small numbers of consecutive pages, to teachers or lecturers, for use with classes in schools or as part of a higher or adult education programme.

2. Publishing facsimiles and transcripts of the returns

Requests for permission to publish parts of the returns, in facsimile or transcript, should be addressed to the Copyright Officer at the Public Record Office, who will, in most instances, be able to give permission for the project. The PRO reserves the right to levy Crown copyright reproduction fees, although such fees are not normally charged for non-profit-making publications by individuals or by family and local history societies. Proposals for publication on a large or highly commercial scale, and proposals to reproduce the contents of the returns for distribution in machine readable form, may be referred to Her Majesty's Stationery Office, which bears ultimate responsibility for the administration of Crown copyright.

Requests for permission to publish should be made in writing, and should always include full details of the proposed publication, and the PRO document reference(s) of the returns concerned. These references are clearly visible on all microfilm copies of the census returns.

3. Publishing indexes to the returns

Permission is not always required for the publication of indexes to the returns. Copyright is infringed only if the information in the returns is reproduced exactly, or so completely that the new work becomes a substitute for the originals. This means that there is no potential infringement, and hence no need for permission, if all that is to be published is a simple index which serves only as a finding aid to the returns. An example of this would be a surname index referring users to a particular entry, which they would then need to consult on microfilm for full details.

N.B. Any work which contains all the information given in the original returns counts as full reproduction for which permission is required, even if the information has been rearranged in the transcript (eg in alphabetical order of surname).

4. The 1881 Microfiche Project

Two distinct copyrights subsist in the microfiche indexes to the 1881 census. The data from the returns are Crown copyright: copyright in the indexes themselves, including their arrangement and layout, belongs to the Church of Jesus Christ of the Latter-Day Saints. Both copyright owners are happy that limited numbers of copies (both fiche and hard copy) should be made from the microfiche edition, in the quantities and for the purposes outlined in paragraph 1 above. Requests for permission to produce or obtain more extensive quantities of copies, or for permission to publish any portion of the indexes in facsimile or transcript, should be addressed in the first instance to the copyright officer of the Church. Some requests may be referred subsequently to HM Stationery Office.

APPENDIX 4 PLAN OF THE REFERENCE ROOMS, CHANCERY LANE

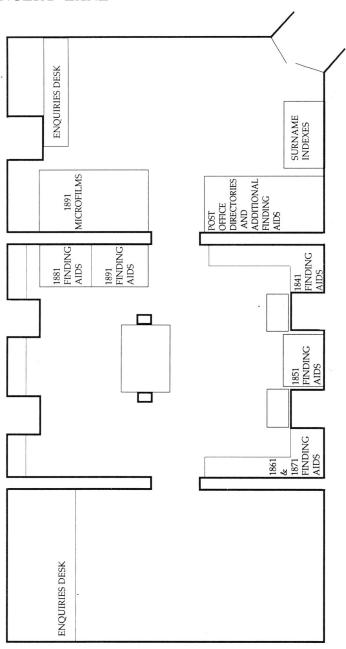

APPENDIX 5   PLAN OF THE CENSUS ROOM, CHANCERY LANE

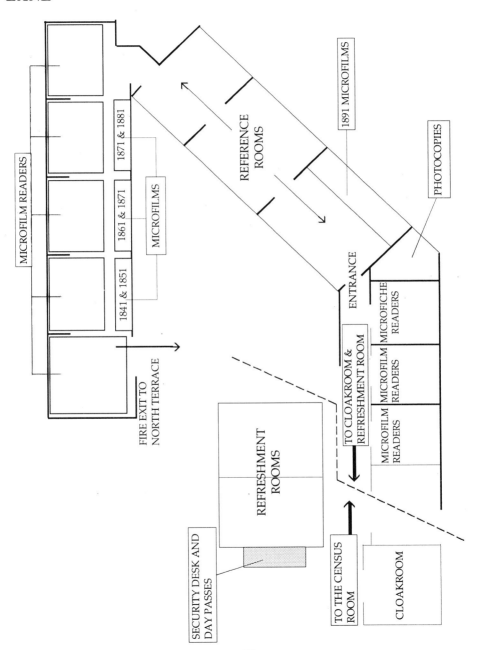

APPENDIX 6   DOCUMENT REFERENCES

Reference numbers are needed to identify specific documents, not just census returns, and have three component parts. The first is the letter code to the group of documents into which your particular document falls. This letter code relates to the government department which transferred the document. In the case of the census this is HO (Home Office) for 1841 and 1851 and RG (Registrar General) for all other years.

The second part is a class number, since each group of documents is subdivided into classes relating to different types of documents all being transferred from the same source. To cite an example, the classes of the RG group are as follows: RG 1-3 are the indexes to the birth, marriage and death registers still held at St Catherine's House, 10 Kingsway, London WC2B 6JP; RG 4 nonconformist registers (gathered in 1837); RG 5 certificates of Dr Williams' Library; RG 6 Quaker registers; RG 7 Fleet marriage registers; RG 8 unauthenticated nonconformist registers (gathered in 1857); RG 9 1861 census returns; RG 10 1871 census returns; RG 11 1881 census returns; RG 12 1891 census returns and so on. RG 18 reference maps of registrar's districts, RG 19 correspondence and papers, RG 27 specimens of forms and documents and RG 30 reports and population abstracts, are some of the later classes.

The third part of the reference is what is known as a piece number. This is simply an archival term for an individual item which may take many shapes and forms, but which when relating to the census means an enumerator's folder or in 1841 and 1851 a box of these folders.

To complete a reference you need to add the particular folio number or numbers followed by either recto or verso, or a page number.   See page 56 for a fuller explanation of this.

These document references are universal in that they are present on a reel of census microfilm wherever you view it. However, if you are looking at the census away from the PRO in a local record office or a family history library, you will not have the same finding aids available to identify your part of the census in the same way. Quite naturally other search rooms have their own collections and will need to add any purchased microfilms to their own holdings. This means that a new reference will need to be applied to any item purchased by them in order for it to be added to their referencing system. Local record offices in particular may have also purchased copies of street indexes, where available, from the PRO so that PRO references can be used in conjunction with their own system. Taking with you to another record office a PRO reference number may therefore necessitate an extra exercise before you can find your film. The local archivist or search room officer should be able to help you do this. Once you have found your place on the film you will be able to refer back to it by the method described on page 56. Similarly the local referencing system will not be intelligible away from its own collection so you will need the PRO reference for what you wish to record to make it universally intelligible.

APPENDIX 7 REGISTRATION DISTRICTS

1851		1861		1871		1881		1891	
	pt Kensington		pt Kensington		pt Kensington		pt Kensington	1A	Paddington
1	Kensington	1	Kensington	1	Kensington	1	Kensington	1B	Kensington
	pt Kensington		pt Kensington		pt Kensington	2	Fulham	2	Fulham
2	Chelsea	2	Chelsea	2	Chelsea	3	Chelsea	3	Chelsea
3	St George Hanover Sq	3	St George Hanover Sq	3	St George Hanover Sq	4	St George Hanover Sq	4	St George Hanover Sq
4	Westminster	4	Westminster	4	Westminster	5	Westminster	5	Westminster
5	St Martin in the Fields	5	St Martin in the Fields		pt Westminster		pt Westminster		pt Westminster
6	St James Westminster	6	St James Westminster		pt Westminster		pt Westminster		pt Westminster
7	Marylebone	7	Marylebone	5	Marylebone	6	Marylebone	6	Marylebone
8	Hampstead	8	Hampstead	6	Hampstead	7	Hampstead	7	Hampstead
9	Pancras	9	Pancras	7	Pancras	8	Pancras	8	Pancras
10	Islington	10	Islington	8	Islington	9	Islington	9	Islington
11	Hackney	11	Hackney	9	Hackney	10	Hackney	10	Hackney
12	St Giles	12	St Giles	10	St Giles	11	St Giles	11	St Giles
13	Strand	13	Strand	11	Strand	12	Strand	12	Strand
14	Holborn	14	Holborn	12	Holborn	13	Holborn	13	Holborn
15	Clerkenwell	15	Clerkenwell		pt Holborn		pt Holborn		pt Holborn
16	St Luke	16	St Luke		pt Holborn		pt Holborn		pt Holborn
17	E London	17	E London		pt London City		pt London City		pt London City
18	W London	18	W London		pt London City		pt London City		pt London City
19	London City	19	London City	13	London City	14	London City	14	London City
20	Shoreditch	20	Shoreditch	14	Shoreditch	15	Shoreditch	15	Shoreditch
21	Bethnal Green	21	Bethnal Green	15	Bethnal Green	16	Bethnal Green	16	Bethnal Green
22	Whitechapel	22	Whitechapel	16	Whitechapel	17	Whitechapel	17	Whitechapel
23	St George in the East	23	St George in the East	17	St George in the East	18	St George in the East	18	St George in the East
24	Stepney	24A	Stepney	18	Stepney	19	Stepney	19	Stepney
	pt Stepney	24B	Mile End Old Town	19	Mile End Old Town	20	Mile End Old Town	20	Mile End Old Town

1851	1861	1871	1881	1891
25 Poplar	25 Poplar	20 Poplar	21 Poplar	21 Poplar
26 St Saviour Southwark	26 St Saviour Southwark	21 St Saviour Southwark	22 St Saviour Southwark	22 St Saviour Southwark
27 St Olave Southwark	27 St Olave Southwark	22 St Olave Southwark	23 St Olave Southwark	23 St Olave Southwark
28 Bermondsey	28 Bermondsey	pt St Olave	pt St Olave	pt St Olave
29 St George Southwark	29 St George Southwark	pt St Saviour	pt St Saviour	pt St Saviour
30 Newington	30 Newington	pt St Saviour	pt St Saviour	pt St Saviour
31 Lambeth	31 Lambeth	23 Lambeth	24 Lambeth	24 Lambeth
32 Wandsworth	32 Wandsworth	24 Wandsworth	25 Wandsworth	25 Wandsworth
33 Camberwell	33 Camberwell	25 Camberwell	26 Camberwell	26 Camberwell
34 Rotherhithe	34 Rotherhithe	pt St Olave	pt St Olave	pt St Olave
35 Greenwich	35 Greenwich	26 Greenwich	27 Greenwich	27 Greenwich
36 Lewisham	36 Lewisham	27 Lewisham	28 Lewisham	28 Lewisham
pt Greenwich	pt Greenwich	28 Woolwich	29 Woolwich	29 Woolwich
37 Epsom	37 Epsom	29 Epsom	30 Epsom	30 Epsom
38 Chertsey	38 Chertsey	30 Chertsey	31 Chertsey	31 Chertsey
39 Guildford	39 Guildford	31 Guildford	32 Guildford	32 Guildford
40 Farnham	40 Farnham	32 Farnham	33 Farnham	33 Farnham
41 Farnborough	41 Farnborough	pt Hartley Wintney	pt Hartley Wintney	pt Hartley Wintney
42 Hambledon	42 Hambledon	33 Hambledon	34 Hambledon	34 Hambledon
43 Dorking	43 Dorking	34 Dorking	35 Dorking	35 Dorking
44 Reigate	44 Reigate	35 Reigate	36 Reigate	36 Reigate
45 Godstone	45 Godstone	36 Godstone	37 Godstone	37 Godstone
46 Croydon	46 Croydon	37 Croydon	38 Croydon	38 Croydon
47 Kingston	47 Kingston	38 Kingston	39 Kingston	39 Kingston
48 Richmond	48 Richmond	39 Richmond	40 Richmond	40 Richmond
49 Bromley	49 Bromley	40 Bromley	41 Bromley	41 Bromley
50 Dartford	50 Dartford	41 Dartford	42 Dartford	42 Dartford
51 Gravesend	51 Gravesend	42 Gravesend	43 Gravesend	43 Gravesend

1851		1861		1871		1881		1891	
52	North Aylesford	52	North Aylesford	43	North Aylesford	44	North Aylesford	44	Strood
53	Hoo	53	Hoo	44	Hoo	45	Hoo	45	Hoo
54	Medway	54	Medway	45	Medway	46	Medway	46	Medway
55	Malling	55	Malling	46	Malling	47	Malling	47	Malling
56	Sevenoaks	56	Sevenoaks	47	Sevenoaks	48	Sevenoaks	48	Sevenoaks
57	Tonbridge	57	Tonbridge	48	Tonbridge	49	Tonbridge	49	Tonbridge
58	Maidstone	58	Maidstone	49	Maidstone	50	Maidstone	50	Maidstone
59	Hollingbourne	59	Hollingbourne	50	Hollingbourne	51	Hollingbourne	51	Hollingbourne
60	Cranbrook	60	Cranbrook	51	Cranbrook	52	Cranbrook	52	Cranbrook
61	Tenterden	61	Tenterden	52	Tenterden	53	Tenterden	53	Tenterden
62	West Ashford	62	West Ashford	53	West Ashford	54	West Ashford	54	West Ashford
63	East Ashford	63	East Ashford	54	East Ashford	55	East Ashford	55	East Ashford
64	Bridge	64	Bridge	55	Bridge	56	Bridge	56	Bridge
65	Canterbury	65	Canterbury	56	Canterbury	57	Canterbury	57	Canterbury
66	Blean	66	Blean	57	Blean	58	Blean	58	Blean
67	Faversham	67	Faversham	58	Faversham	59	Faversham	59	Faversham
68	Milton	68	Milton	59	Milton	60	Milton	60	Milton
69	Sheppey	69	Sheppey	60	Sheppey	61	Sheppey	61	Sheppey
70	Thanet	70	Thanet	61	Thanet	62	Thanet	62	Thanet
71	Eastry	71	Eastry	62	Eastry	63	Eastry	63	Eastry
72	Dover	72	Dover	63	Dover	64	Dover	64	Dover
73	Elham	73	Elham	64	Elham	65	Elham	65	Elham
74	Romney Marsh	74	Romney Marsh	65	Romney Marsh	66	Romney Marsh	66	Romney Marsh
75	Rye	75	Rye	66	Rye	67	Rye	67	Rye
76	Hastings	76	Hastings	67	Hastings	68	Hastings	68	Hastings
77	Battle	77	Battle	68	Battle	69	Battle	69	Battle
78	Eastbourne	78	Eastbourne	69	Eastbourne	70	Eastbourne	70	Eastbourne

1851		1861		1871		1881		1891	
80	Ticehurst	80	Ticehurst	71	Ticehurst	72	Ticehurst	72	Ticehurst
81	Uckfield	81	Uckfield	72	Uckfield	73	Uckfield	73	Uckfield
82	East Grinstead	82	East Grinstead	73	East Grinstead	74	East Grinstead	74	East Grinstead
83	Cuckfield	83	Cuckfield	74	Cuckfield	75	Cuckfield	75	Cuckfield
84	Lewes	84	Lewes	75	Lewes	76	Lewes	76	Lewes
85	Brighton	85	Brighton	76	Brighton	77	Brighton	77	Brighton
86	Steyning	86	Steyning	77	Steyning	78	Steyning	78	Steyning
87	Horsham	87	Horsham	78	Horsham	79	Horsham	79	Horsham
88	Petworth	88	Petworth	79	Petworth	80	Petworth	80	Petworth
89	Thakeham	89	Thakeham	80	Thakeham	81	Thakeham	81	Thakeham
	pt Worthing		pt Worthing	81	East Preston	82	East Preston	82	East Preston
90	Worthing	90	Worthing		pt East Preston		pt East Preston		pt East Preston
91	Westhampnett	91	Westhampnett	82	Westhampnett	83	Westhampnett	83	Westhampnett
92	Chichester	92	Chichester	83	Chichester	84	Chichester	84	Chichester
93	Midhurst	93	Midhurst	84	Midhurst	85	Midhurst	85	Midhurst
94	Westbourne	94	Westbourne	85	Westbourne	86	Westbourne	86	Westbourne
95	Havant	95	Havant	86	Havant	87	Havant	87	Havant
96	Portsea Island	96	Portsea Island	87	Portsea Island	88	Portsea Island	88	Portsea Island
97	Alverstoke	97	Alverstoke	88	Alverstoke	89	Alverstoke	89	Alverstoke
98	Fareham	98	Fareham	89	Fareham	90	Fareham	90	Fareham
99	Isle of Wight	99	Isle of Wight	90	Isle of Wight	91	Isle of Wight	91	Isle of Wight
100	Lymington	100	Lymington	91	Lymington	92	Lymington	92	Lymington
101	Christchurch	101	Christchurch	92	Christchurch	93	Christchurch	93	Christchurch
102	Ringwood	102	Ringwood	93	Ringwood	94	Ringwood	94	Ringwood
103	Fordingbridge	103	Fordingbridge	94	Fordingbridge	95	Fordingbridge	95	Fordingbridge
104	New Forest	104	New Forest	95	New Forest	96	New Forest	96	New Forest
105	Southampton	105	Southampton	96	Southampton	97	Southampton	97	Southampton
106	South Stoneham	106	South Stoneham	97	South Stoneham	98	South Stoneham	98	South Stoneham

District	1851	1861	1871	1881	1891
Romsey	107	107	98	99	99
Stockbridge	108	108	99	100	100
Winchester	109	109	100	101	101
Droxford	110	110	101	102	102
Catherington	111	111	102	103	103
Petersfield	112	112	103	104	104
Alresford	113	113	104	105	105
Alton	114	114	105	106	106
Hartley Wintney	115	115	106	107	107
Basingstoke	116	116	107	108	108
Whitchurch	117	117	108	109	109
Andover	118	118	109	110	110
Kingsclere	119	119	110	111	111
Newbury	120	120	111	112	112
Hungerford	121	121	112	113	113
Faringdon	122	122	113	114	114
Abingdon	123	123	114	115	115
Wantage	124	124	115	116	116
Wallingford	125	125	116	117	117
Bradfield	126	126	117	118	118
Reading	127	127	118	119	119
Wokingham	128	128	119	120	120
Cookham	129	129	120	121	121
Easthampstead	130	130	121	122	122
Windsor	131	131	122	123	123
Staines	132	132	123	124	124
Uxbridge	133	133	124	125	125
Brentford	134	134	125.	126	126

Place	1851	1861	1871	1881	1891
Hendon	135	135	126	127	127
Barnet	136	136	127	128	128
Edmonton	137	137	128	129	129
Ware	138	138	129	130	130
Bishops Stortford	139	139	130	131	131
Royston	140	140	131	132	132
Hitchin	141	141	132	133	133
Hertford	142	142	133	134	134
Hatfield	143	143	134	135	135
St Albans	144	144	135	136	136
Watford	145	145	136	137	137
Hemel Hempstead	146	146	137	138*	138
Berkhamsted	147	147	138	139	139
Amersham	148	148	139	140	140
Eton	149	149	140	141	141
Wycombe	150	150	141	142	142
Aylesbury	151	151	142	143	143
Winslow	152	152	143	144	144
Newport Pagnell	153	153	144	145	145
Buckingham	154	154	145	146	146
Henley	155	155	146	147	147
Thame	156	156	147	148	148
Headington	157	157	148	149	149
Oxford	158	158	149	150	150
Bicester	159	159	150	151	151
Woodstock	160	160	151	152	152
Witney	161	161	152	153	153
Chipping Norton	162	162	153	154	154

1851	1861	1871	1881	1891
163 Banbury	163 Banbury	154 Banbury	155 Banbury	155 Banbury
164 Brackley	164 Brackley	155 Brackley	156 Brackley	156 Brackley
165 Towcester	165 Towcester	156 Towcester	157 Towcester	157 Towcester
166 Potterspury	166 Potterspury	157 Potterspury	158 Potterspury	158 Potterspury
167 Hardingstone	167 Hardingstone	158 Hardingstone	159 Hardingstone	159 Hardingstone
168 Northampton	168 Northampton	159 Northampton	160 Northampton	160 Northampton
169 Daventry	169 Daventry	160 Daventry	161 Daventry	161 Daventry
170 Brixworth	170 Brixworth	161 Brixworth	162 Brixworth	162 Brixworth
171 Wellingborough	171 Wellingborough	162 Wellingborough	163 Wellingborough	163 Wellingborough
172 Kettering	172 Kettering	163 Kettering	164 Kettering	164 Kettering
173 Thrapston	173 Thrapston	164 Thrapston	165 Thrapston	165 Thrapston
174 Oundle	174 Oundle	165 Oundle	166 Oundle	166 Oundle
175 Peterborough	175 Peterborough	166 Peterborough	167 Peterborough	167 Peterborough
176 Huntingdon	176 Huntingdon	167 Huntingdon	168 Huntingdon	168 Huntingdon
177 St Ives	177 St Ives	168 St Ives	169 St Ives	169 St Ives
178 St Neots	178 St Neots	169 St Neots	170 St Neots	170 St Neots
179 Bedford	179 Bedford	170 Bedford	171 Bedford	171 Bedford
180 Biggleswade	180 Biggleswade	171 Biggleswade	172 Biggleswade	172 Biggleswade
181 Ampthill	181 Ampthill	172 Ampthill	173 Ampthill	173 Ampthill
182 Woburn	182 Woburn	173 Woburn	174 Woburn	174 Woburn
183 Leighton Buzzard	183 Leighton Buzzard	174 Leighton Buzzard	175 Leighton Buzzard	175 Leighton Buzzard
184 Luton	184 Luton	175 Luton	176 Luton	176 Luton
185 Caxton	185 Caxton	176 Caxton	177 Caxton	177 Caxton
186 Chesterton	186 Chesterton	177 Chesterton	178 Chesterton	178 Chesterton
187 Cambridge	187 Cambridge	178 Cambridge	179 Cambridge	179 Cambridge
188 Linton	188 Linton	179 Linton	180 Linton	180 Linton
189 Newmarket	189 Newmarket	180 Newmarket	181 Newmarket	181 Newmarket
190 Ely	190 Ely	181 Ely	182 Ely	182 Ely

1851		1861		1871		1881		1891	
191	North Witchford	191	North Witchford	182	North Witchford	183	North Witchford	183	North Witchford
192	Whittlesey	192	Whittlesey	183	Whittlesey	184	Whittlesey	184	Whittlesey
193	Wisbech	193	Wisbech	184	Wisbech	185	Wisbech	185	Wisbech
194	West Ham	194	West Ham	185	West Ham	186	West Ham	186	West Ham
195	Epping	195	Epping	186	Epping	187	Epping	187	Epping
196	Ongar	196	Ongar	187	Ongar	188	Ongar	188	Ongar
197	Romford	197	Romford	188	Romford	189	Romford	189	Romford
198	Orsett	198	Orsett	189	Orsett	190	Orsett	190	Orsett
199	Billericay	199	Billericay	190	Billericay	191	Billericay	191	Billericay
200	Chelmsford	200	Chelmsford	191	Chelmsford	192	Chelmsford	192	Chelmsford
201	Rochford	201	Rochford	192	Rochford	193	Rochford	193	Rochford
202	Maldon	202	Maldon	193	Maldon	194	Maldon	194	Maldon
203	Tendring	203	Tendring	194	Tendring	195	Tendring	195	Tendring
204	Colchester	204	Colchester	195	Colchester	196	Colchester	196	Colchester
205	Lexden	205	Lexden	196	Lexden	197	Lexden	197	Lexden
206	Witham	206	Witham	197	Witham		pt Lexden		pt Lexden
207	Halstead	207	Halstead	198	Halstead	198	Halstead	198	Halstead
208	Braintree	208	Braintree	199	Braintree	199	Braintree	199	Braintree
209	Dunmow	209	Dunmow	200	Dunmow	200	Dunmow	200	Dunmow
210	Saffron Walden	210	Saffron Walden	201	Saffron Walden	201	Saffron Walden	201	Saffron Walden
211	Risbridge	211	Risbridge	202	Risbridge	202	Risbridge	202	Risbridge
212	Sudbury	212	Sudbury	203	Sudbury	203	Sudbury	203	Sudbury
213	Cosford	213	Cosford	204	Cosford	204	Cosford	204	Cosford
214	Thingoe	214	Thingoe	205	Thingoe	205	Thingoe	205	Thingoe
215	Bury St Edmunds	215	Bury St Edmunds	206	Bury St Edmunds	206	Bury St Edmunds	206	Bury St Edmunds
216	Mildenhall	216	Mildenhall	207	Mildenhall	207	Mildenhall	207	Mildenhall
217	Stow	217	Stow	208	Stow	208	Stow	208	Stow
218	Hartismere	218	Hartismere	209	Hartismere	209	Hartismere	209	Hartismere

1851		1861		1871		1881		1891	
219	Hoxne	219	Hoxne	210	Hoxne	210	Hoxne	210	Hoxne
220	Bosmere	220	Bosmere	211	Bosmere	211	Bosmere	211	Bosmere
221	Samford	221	Samford	212	Samford	212	Samford	212	Samford
222	Ipswich	222	Ipswich	213	Ipswich	213	Ipswich	213	Ipswich
223	Woodbridge	223	Woodbridge	214	Woodbridge	214	Woodbridge	214	Woodbridge
224	Plomesgate	224	Plomesgate	215	Plomesgate	215	Plomesgate	215	Plomesgate
225	Blything	225	Blything	216	Blything	216	Blything	216	Blything
226	Wangford	226	Wangford	217	Wangford	217	Wangford	217	Wangford
227	Mutford	227	Mutford	218	Mutford	218	Mutford	218	Mutford
228	Yarmouth	228	Yarmouth	219	Yarmouth	219	Yarmouth	219	Yarmouth
229	Flegg	229	Flegg	220	Flegg	220	Flegg	220	Flegg
230	Tunstead	230	Tunstead	221	Smallburgh	221	Smallburgh	221	Smallburgh
231	Erpingham	231	Erpingham	222	Erpingham	222	Erpingham	222	Erpingham
232	Aylsham	232	Aylsham	223	Aylsham	223	Aylsham	223	Aylsham
233	St Faith's	233	St Faith's	224	St Faith's	224	St Faith's	224	St Faith's
234	Norwich	234	Norwich	225	Norwich	225	Norwich	225	Norwich
235	Forehoe	235	Forehoe	226	Forehoe	226	Forehoe	226	Forehoe
236	Henstead	236	Henstead	227	Henstead	227	Henstead	227	Henstead
237	Blofield	237	Blofield	228	Blofield	228	Blofield	228	Blofield
238	Loddon	238	Loddon	229	Loddon	229	Loddon	229	Loddon
239	Depwade	239	Depwade	230	Depwade	230	Depwade	230	Depwade
240	Guiltcross	240	Guiltcross	231	Guiltcross	231	Guiltcross	231	Guiltcross
241	Wayland	241	Wayland	232	Wayland	232	Wayland	232	Wayland
242	Mitford	242	Mitford	233	Mitford	233	Mitford	233	Mitford
243	Walsingham	243	Walsingham	234	Walsingham	234	Walsingham	234	Walsingham
244	Docking	244	Docking	235	Docking	235	Docking	235	Docking
245	Freebridge Lynn	245	Freebridge Lynn	236	Freebridge Lynn	236	Freebridge Lynn	236	Freebridge Lynn
246	King's Lynn	246	King's Lynn	237	King's Lynn	237	King's Lynn	237	King's Lynn

1851	1861	1871	1881	1891
247 Downham	247 Downham	238 Downham	238 Downham	238 Downham
248 Swaffham	248 Swaffham	239 Swaffham	239 Swaffham	239 Swaffham
249 Thetford	249 Thetford	240 Thetford	240 Thetford	240 Thetford
250 Highworth	250 Highworth	241 Highworth	241 Highworth	241 Highworth
251 Cricklade	251 Cricklade	242 Cricklade	242 Cricklade	242 Cricklade
252 Malmesbury	252 Malmesbury	243 Malmesbury	243 Malmesbury	243 Malmesbury
253 Chippenham	253 Chippenham	244 Chippenham	244 Chippenham	244 Chippenham
254 Calne	254 Calne	245 Calne	245 Calne	245 Calne
255 Marlborough	255 Marlborough	246 Marlborough	246 Marlborough	246 Marlborough
256 Devizes	256 Devizes	247 Devizes	247 Devizes	247 Devizes
257 Melksham	257 Melksham	248 Melksham	248 Melksham	248 Melksham
258 Bradford on Avon	258 Bradford on Avon	249 Bradford on Avon	249 Bradford on Avon	249 Bradford on Avon
259 Westbury	259 Westbury	250 Westbury	250 Westbury	250 Westbury
260 Warminster	260 Warminster	251 Warminster	251 Warminster	251 Warminster
261 Pewsey	261 Pewsey	252 Pewsey	252 Pewsey	252 Pewsey
262 Amesbury	262 Amesbury	253 Amesbury	253 Amesbury	253 Amesbury
263 Alderbury	263 Alderbury	254 Alderbury	254 Alderbury	254 Alderbury
264 Salisbury	264 Salisbury	pt Alderbury	pt Alderbury	pt Alderbury
265 Wilton	265 Wilton	255 Wilton	255 Wilton	255 Wilton
266 Tisbury	266 Tisbury	256 Tisbury	256 Tisbury	256 Tisbury
267 Mere	267 Mere	257 Mere	257 Mere	257 Mere
268 Shaftesbury	268 Shaftesbury	258 Shaftesbury	258 Shaftesbury	258 Shaftesbury
269 Sturminster	269 Sturminster	259 Sturminster	259 Sturminster	259 Sturminster
270 Blandford	270 Blandford	260 Blandford	260 Blandford	260 Blandford
271 Wimborne	271 Wimborne	261 Wimborne	261 Wimborne	261 Wimborne
272 Poole	272 Poole	262 Poole	262 Poole	262 Poole
273 Wareham	273 Wareham	263 Wareham	263 Wareham	263 Wareham
274 Weymouth	274 Weymouth	264 Weymouth	264 Weymouth	264 Weymouth

1851	1861	1871	1881	1891	District
275	275	265	265	265	Dorchester
276	276	266	266	266	Sherborne
277	277	267	267	267	Beaminster
278	278	268	268	268	Bridport
279	279	269	269	269	Axminster
280	280	270	270	270	Honiton
281	281	271	271	271	St Thomas
282	282	272	272	272	Exeter
283	283	273	273	273	Newton Abbot
284	284	274	274	274	Totnes
285	285	275	275	275	Kingsbridge
286	286	276	276	276	Plympton St Mary
287	287	277	277	277	Plymouth
288	288	278	278	278	East Stonehouse
289	289	279	279	279	Stoke Damerel
290	290	280	280	280	Tavistock
291	291	281	281	281	Okehampton
292	292	282	282	282	Crediton
293	293	283	283	283	Tiverton
294	294	284	284	284	South Molton
295	295	285	285	285	Barnstaple
296	296	286	286	286	Torrington
297	297	287	287	287	Bideford
298	298	288	288	288	Holsworthy
299	299	289	289	289	Stratton
300	300	290	290	290	Camelford
301	301	291	291	291	Launceston
302	302	292	292	292	St Germans

1851		1861		1871		1881		1891	
303	Liskeard	303	Liskeard	293	Liskeard	293	Liskeard	293	Liskeard
304	Bodmin	304	Bodmin	294	Bodmin	294	Bodmin	294	Bodmin
305	St Columb	305	St Columb	295	St Columb	295	St Columb	295	St Columb
306	St Austell	306	St Austell	296	St Austell	296	St Austell	296	St Austell
307	Truro	307	Truro	297	Truro	297	Truro	297	Truro
308	Falmouth	308	Falmouth	298	Falmouth	298	Falmouth	298	Falmouth
309	Helston	309	Helston	299	Helston	299	Helston	299	Helston
310	Redruth	310	Redruth	300	Redruth	300	Redruth	300	Redruth
311	Penzance	311	Penzance	301	Penzance	301	Penzance	301	Penzance
312	Scilly Isles	312	Scilly Isles	302	Scilly Isles	302	Scilly Isles	302	Scilly Isles
313	Williton	313A	Williton	303	Williton	303	Williton	303	Williton
	pt Tiverton	313B	Dulverton	304	Dulverton	304	Dulverton	304	Dulverton
314	Wellington	314	Wellington	305	Wellington	305	Wellington	305	Wellington
315	Taunton	315	Taunton	306	Taunton	306	Taunton	306	Taunton
316	Bridgwater	316	Bridgwater	307	Bridgwater	307	Bridgwater	307	Bridgwater
317	Langport	317	Langport	308	Langport	308	Langport	308	Langport
318	Chard	318	Chard	309	Chard	309	Chard	309	Chard
319	Yeovil	319	Yeovil	310	Yeovil	310	Yeovil	310	Yeovil
320	Wincanton	320	Wincanton	311	Wincanton	311	Wincanton	311	Wincanton
321	Frome	321	Frome	312	Frome	312	Frome	312	Frome
322	Shepton Mallet	322	Shepton Mallet	313	Shepton Mallet	313	Shepton Mallet	313	Shepton Mallet
323	Wells	323	Wells	314	Wells	314	Wells	314	Wells
324	Axbridge	324	Axbridge	315	Axbridge	315	Axbridge	315	Axbridge
325	Clutton	325	Clutton	316	Clutton	316	Clutton	316	Clutton
326	Bath	326	Bath	317	Bath	317	Bath	317	Bath
327	Keynsham	327	Keynsham	318	Keynsham	318	Keynsham	318	Keynsham
328	Bedminster	328	Bedminster	319	Bedminster	319	Bedminster	319	Bedminster
329	Bristol	329	Bristol	320	Bristol	320	Bristol	320	Bristol

1851		1861		1871		1881		1891	
330	Clifton	330	Clifton	321	Clifton	321	Clifton	321	Barton Regis
331	Chipping Sodbury	331	Chipping Sodbury	322	Chipping Sodbury	322	Chipping Sodbury	322	Chipping Sodbury
332	Thornbury	332	Thornbury	323	Thornbury	323	Thornbury	323	Thornbury
333	Dursley	333	Dursley	324	Dursley	324	Dursley	324	Dursley
334	Westbury on Severn	334	Westbury on Severn	325	Westbury on Severn	325	Westbury on Severn	325	Westbury on Severn
335	Newent	335	Newent	326	Newent	326	Newent	326	Newent
336	Gloucester	336	Gloucester	327	Gloucester	327	Gloucester	327	Gloucester
337	Wheatenhurst	337	Wheatenhurst	328	Wheatenhurst	328	Wheatenhurst	328	Wheatenhurst
338	Stroud	338	Stroud	329	Stroud	329	Stroud	329	Stroud
339	Tetbury	339	Tetbury	330	Tetbury	330	Tetbury	330	Tetbury
340	Cirencester	340	Cirencester	331	Cirencester	331	Cirencester	331	Cirencester
341	Northleach	341	Northleach	332	Northleach	332	Northleach	332	Northleach
342	Stow-on-the-Wold	342	Stow on the Wold	333	Stow on the Wold	333	Stow on the Wold	333	Stow on the Wold
343	Winchcomb	343	Winchcomb	334	Winchcomb	334	Winchcomb	334	Winchcomb
344	Cheltenham	344	Cheltenham	335	Cheltenham	335	Cheltenham	335	Cheltenham
345	Tewkesbury	345	Tewkesbury	336	Tewkesbury	336	Tewkesbury	336	Tewkesbury
346	Ledbury	346	Ledbury	337	Ledbury	337	Ledbury	337	Ledbury
347	Ross	347	Ross	338	Ross	338	Ross	338	Ross
348	Hereford	348	Hereford	339	Hereford	339	Hereford	339	Hereford
349	Weobly	349	Weobley	340	Weobley	340	Weobley	340	Weobley
350	Bromyard	350	Bromyard	341	Bromyard	341	Bromyard	341	Bromyard
351	Leominster	351	Leominster	342	Leominster	342	Leominster	342	Leominster
	pt Presteigne		pt Presteigne	343	Kington	343	Kington	343	Kington
352	Ludlow	352	Ludlow	344	Ludlow	344	Ludlow	344	Ludlow
353	Clun	353	Clun	345	Clun	345	Clun	345	Clun
354	Church Stretton	354	Church Stretton	346	Church Stretton	346	Church Stretton	346	Church Stretton
355	Cleobury Mortimer	355	Cleobury Mortimer	347	Cleobury Mortimer	347	Cleobury Mortimer	347	Cleobury Mortimer
356	Bridgnorth	356	Bridgnorth	348	Bridgnorth	348	Bridgnorth	348	Bridgnorth

1851		1861		1871		1881		1891	
357	Shifnal	357	Shifnal	349	Shifnal	349	Shifnal	349	Shifnal
358	Madeley	358	Madeley	350	Madeley	350	Madeley	350	Madeley
359	Atcham	359	Atcham	351	Atcham	351	Atcham	351	Atcham
							pt Atcham		pt Atcham
360	Shrewsbury	360	Shrewsbury	352	Shrewsbury				
361	Oswestry	361	Oswestry	353	Oswestry	352	Oswestry	352	Oswestry
362	Ellesmere	362	Ellesmere	354	Ellesmere	353	Ellesmere	353	Ellesmere
363	Wem	363A	Wem	355	Wem	354	Wem	354	Wem
	pt Wem								
		363B	Whitchurch	356	Whitchurch	355	Whitchurch	355	Whitchurch
364	Market Drayton	364	Market Drayton	357	Market Drayton	356	Market Drayton	356	Market Drayton
365	Wellington	365	Wellington	358	Wellington	357	Wellington	357	Wellington
366	Newport	366	Newport	359	Newport	358	Newport	358	Newport
367	Stafford	367	Stafford	360	Stafford	359	Stafford	359	Stafford
368	Stone	368	Stone	361	Stone	360	Stone	360	Stone
369	Newcastle under Lyme	369	Newcastle under Lyme	362	Newcastle under Lyme	361	Newcastle under Lyme	361	Newcastle under Lyme
370	Wolstanton	370	Wolstanton	363	Wolstanton	362	Wolstanton	362	Wolstanton
371	Stoke on Trent	371	Stoke on Trent	364	Stoke on Trent	363	Stoke on Trent	363	Stoke on Trent
372	Leek	372	Leek	365	Leek	364	Leek	364	Leek
373	Cheadle	373	Cheadle	366	Cheadle	365	Cheadle	365	Cheadle
374	Uttoxeter	374	Uttoxeter	367	Uttoxeter	366	Uttoxeter	366	Uttoxeter
375	Burton upon Trent	375	Burton upon Trent	368	Burton upon Trent	367	Burton upon Trent	367	Burton-upon-Trent
376	Tamworth	376	Tamworth	369	Tamworth	368	Tamworth	368	Tamworth
377	Lichfield	377	Lichfield	370	Lichfield	369	Lichfield	369	Lichfield
378	Penkridge	378	Penkridge	371	Penkridge	370	Cannock	370	Cannock
379	Wolverhampton	379	Wolverhampton	372	Wolverhampton	371	Wolverhampton	371	Wolverhampton
380	Walsall	380	Walsall	373	Walsall	372	Walsall	372	Walsall
381	West Bromwich	381	West Bromwich	374	West Bromwich	373	West Bromwich	373	West Bromwich
382	Dudley	382	Dudley	375	Dudley	374	Dudley	374	Dudley
383	Stourbridge	383	Stourbridge	376	Stourbridge	375	Stourbridge	375	Stourbridge

1851		1861		1871		1881		1891	
384	Kidderminster	384	Kidderminster	377	Kidderminster	376	Kidderminster	376	Kidderminster
385	Tenbury	385	Tenbury	378	Tenbury	377	Tenbury	377	Tenbury
386	Martley	386	Martley	379	Martley	378	Martley	378	Martley
387	Worcester	387	Worcester	380	Worcester	379	Worcester	379	Worcester
388	Upton on Severn	388	Upton on Severn	381	Upton on Severn	380	Upton on Severn	380	Upton on Severn
389	Evesham	389	Evesham	382	Evesham	381	Evesham	381	Evesham
390	Pershore	390	Pershore	383	Pershore	382	Pershore	382	Pershore
391	Droitwich	391	Droitwich	384	Droitwich	383	Droitwich	383	Droitwich
392	Bromsgrove	392	Bromsgrove	385	Bromsgrove	384	Bromsgrove	384	Bromsgrove
393	King's Norton	393	King's Norton	386	King's Norton	385	King's Norton	385	King's Norton
394	Birmingham	394	Birmingham	387	Birmingham	386	Birmingham	386	Birmingham
395	Aston	395	Aston	388	Aston	387	Aston	387	Aston
396	Meriden	396	Meriden	389	Meriden	388	Meriden	388	Meriden
397	Atherstone	397	Atherstone	390	Atherstone	389	Atherstone	389	Atherstone
398	Nuneaton	398	Nuneaton	391	Nuneaton	390	Nuneaton	390	Nuneaton
399	Foleshill	399	Foleshill	392	Foleshill	391	Foleshill	391	Foleshill
400	Coventry	400	Coventry	393	Coventry	392	Coventry	392	Coventry
401	Rugby	401	Rugby	394	Rugby	393	Rugby	393	Rugby
402	Solihull	402	Solihull	395	Solihull	394	Solihull	394	Solihull
403	Warwick	403	Warwick	396	Warwick	395	Warwick	395	Warwick
404	Stratford on Avon	404	Stratford on Avon	397	Stratford on Avon	396	Stratford on Avon	396	Stratford on Avon
405	Alcester	405	Alcester	398	Alcester	397	Alcester	397	Alcester
406	Shipston on Stour	406	Shipston on Stour	399	Shipston on Stour	398	Shipston on Stour	398	Shipston on Stour
407	Southam	407	Southam	400	Southam	399	Southam	399	Southam
408	Lutterworth	408	Lutterworth	401	Lutterworth	400	Lutterworth	400	Lutterworth
409	Market Harborough	409	Market Harborough	402	Market Harborough	401	Market Harborough	401	Market Harborough
410	Billesdon	410	Billesdon	403	Billesdon	402	Billesdon	402	Billesdon
411	Blaby	411	Blaby	404	Blaby	403	Blaby	403	Blaby

District	1851	1861	1871	1881	1891
Hinckley	412	412	405	404	404
Market Bosworth	413	413	406	405	405
Ashby de la Zouch	414	414	407	406	406
Loughborough	415	415	408	407	407
Barrow on Soar	416	416	409	408	408
Leicester	417	417	410	409	409
Melton Mowbray	418	418	411	410	410
Oakham	419	419	412	411	411
Uppingham	420	420	413	412	412
Stamford	421	421	414	413	413
Bourne	422	422	415	414	414
Spalding	423	423	416	415	415
Holbeach	424	424	417	416	416
Boston	425	425	418	417	417
Sleaford	426	426	419	418	418
Grantham	427	427	420	419	419
Lincoln	428	428	421	420	420
Horncastle	429	429	422	421	421
Spilsby	430	430	423	422	422
Louth	431	431	424	423	423
Caistor	432	432	425	424	424
Glanford Brigg	433	433	426	425	425
Gainsborough	434	434	427	426	426
East Retford	435	435	428	427	427
Worksop	436	436	429	428	428
Mansfield	437	437	430	429	429
Basford	438	438	431	430	430
Radford	439	439	432		
pt Nottingham					

92

1851		1861		1871		1881		1891	
440	Nottingham	440	Nottingham	433	Nottingham	431	Nottingham	431	Nottingham
441	Southwell	441	Southwell	434	Southwell	432	Southwell	432	Southwell
442	Newark	442	Newark	435	Newark	433	Newark	433	Newark
443	Bingham	443	Bingham	436	Bingham	434	Bingham	434	Bingham
444	Shardlow	444	Shardlow	437	Shardlow	435	Shardlow	435	Shardlow
445	Derby	445	Derby	438	Derby	436	Derby	436	Derby
446	Belper	446	Belper	439	Belper	437	Belper	437	Belper
447	Ashbourne	447	Ashbourne	440	Ashbourne	438	Ashbourne	438	Ashbourne
448	Chesterfield	448	Chesterfield	441	Chesterfield	439	Chesterfield	439	Chesterfield
449	Bakewell	449	Bakewell	442	Bakewell	440	Bakewell	440	Bakewell
450	Chapel en le Frith	450	Chapel en le Frith	443	Chapel en le Frith	441	Chapel en le Frith	441	Chapel en le Frith
451	Hayfield	451	Hayfield	444	Hayfield	442	Hayfield	442	Hayfield
452	Stockport	452	Stockport	445	Stockport	443	Stockport	443	Stockport
453	Macclesfield	453	Macclesfield	446	Macclesfield	444	Macclesfield	444	Macclesfield
454	Altrincham	454	Altrincham	447	Altrincham	445	Altrincham	445	Altrincham
455	Runcorn	455	Runcorn	448	Runcorn	446	Runcorn	446	Runcorn
456	Northwich	456	Northwich	449	Northwich	447	Northwich	447	Northwich
457	Congleton	457	Congleton	450	Congleton	448	Congleton	448	Congleton
458	Nantwich	458	Nantwich	451	Nantwich	449	Nantwich	449	Nantwich
459	Great Boughton	459	Great Boughton	452	Chester	450	Chester	450	Chester
460	Wirral	460A	Wirral	453	Wirral	451	Wirral	451	Wirral
	pt Wirral	460B	Birkenhead	454	Birkenhead	452	Birkenhead	452	Birkenhead
461	Liverpool	461	Liverpool	455	Liverpool	453	Liverpool	453	Liverpool
	pt Liverpool		pt Liverpool		pt Liverpool	454	Toxteth Park	454	Toxteth Park
462	West Derby	462	West Derby	456	West Derby	455	West Derby	455	West Derby
463	Prescot	463	Prescot	457	Prescot	456	Prescot	456	Prescot
464	Ormskirk	464	Ormskirk	458	Ormskirk	457	Ormskirk	457	Ormskirk
465	Wigan	465	Wigan	459	Wigan	458	Wigan	458	Wigan

1851	1861	1871	1881	1891
466 Warrington	466 Warrington	460 Warrington	459 Warrington	459 Warrington
467 Leigh	467 Leigh	461 Leigh	460 Leigh	460 Leigh
468 Bolton	468 Bolton	462 Bolton	461 Bolton	461 Bolton
469 Bury	469 Bury	463 Bury	462 Bury	462 Bury
470 Barton upon Irwell	470 Barton upon Irwell	464 Barton upon Irwell	463 Barton upon Irwell	463 Barton upon Irwell
471 Chorlton	471 Chorlton	465 Chorlton	464 Chorlton	464 Chorlton
472 Salford	472 Salford	466 Salford	465 Salford	465 Salford
473 Manchester	473 Manchester	467 Manchester	466 Manchester	466 Manchester
pt Manchester	pt Manchester	pt Manchester	467 Prestwich	467 Prestwich
474 Ashton under Lyne	474 Ashton under Lyne	468 Ashton under Lyne	468 Ashton under Lyne	468 Ashton under Lyne
475 Oldham	475 Oldham	469 Oldham	469 Oldham	469 Oldham
476 Rochdale	476 Rochdale	470 Rochdale	470 Rochdale	470 Rochdale
477 Haslingden	477 Haslingden	471 Haslingden	471 Haslingden	471 Haslingden
478 Burnley	478 Burnley	472 Burnley	472 Burnley	472 Burnley
479 Clitheroe	479 Clitheroe	473 Clitheroe	473 Clitheroe	473 Clitheroe
480 Blackburn	480 Blackburn	474 Blackburn	474 Blackburn	474 Blackburn
481 Chorley	481 Chorley	475 Chorley	475 Chorley	475 Chorley
482 Preston	482 Preston	476 Preston	476 Preston	476 Preston
483 Fylde	483 Fylde	477 Fylde	477 Fylde	477 Fylde
484 Garstang	484 Garstang	478 Garstang	478 Garstang	478 Garstang
485 Lancaster	485 Lancaster	479 Lancaster	479 Lancaster	479 Lancaster
pt Lancaster	pt Lancaster	480 Lunesdale	480 Lunesdale	480 Lunesdale
486 Ulverston	486 Ulverston	481 Ulverston	481 Ulverston	481 Ulverston
pt Ulverston	pt Ulverston	pt Ulverston	482 Barrow in Furness	482 Barrow in Furness
487 Sedbergh	487 Sedbergh	482 Sedbergh	483 Sedburgh	483 Sedbergh
488 Settle	488 Settle	483 Settle	484 Settle	484 Settle
489 Skipton	489 Skipton	484 Skipton	485 Skipton	485 Skipton
490 Pateley Bridge	490 Pateley Bridge	485 Pateley Bridge	486 Pateley Bridge	486 Pateley Bridge

1851		1861		1871		1881		1891	
491	Ripon	491	Ripon	486	Ripon	487	Ripon	487	Ripon
	pt Knaresborough	492A	Great Ouseburn	487	Great Ouseburn	488	Great Ouseburn	488	Great Ouseburn
492	Knaresborough	492B	Knaresborough	488	Knaresborough	489	Knaresborough	489	Knaresborough
	pt Knaresborough	492C	Wetherby	489	Wetherby	490	Wetherby	490	Wetherby
	pt Knaresborough	492D	Kirk Deighton		pt Wetherby		pt Wetherby		pt Wetherby
493	Otley	493A	Otley		pt Wharfedale		pt Wharfedale		pt Wharfedale
	pt Otley	493B	Wharfedale	490	Wharfedale	491	Wharfedale	491	Wharfedale
494	Keighley	494	Keighley	491	Keighley	492	Keighley	492	Keighley
495	Todmorden	495	Todmorden	492	Todmorden	493	Todmorden	493	Todmorden
496	Saddleworth	496	Saddleworth	493	Saddleworth	494	Saddleworth	494	Saddleworth
497	Huddersfield	497	Huddersfield	494	Huddersfield	495	Huddersfield	495	Huddersfield
498	Halifax	498	Halifax	495	Halifax	496	Halifax	496	Halifax
499	Bradford	499	Bradford	496	Bradford	497	Bradford	497	Bradford
500	Hunslet	500	Hunslet	497	Hunslet	498	Hunslet	498	Hunslet
	pt Hunslet		pt Hunslet	498	Holbeck	499	Holbeck	499	Holbeck
	pt Hunslet		pt Hunslet	499	Bramley	500	Bramley	500	Bramley
501	Leeds	501	Leeds	500	Leeds	501	Leeds	501	Leeds
502	Dewsbury	502	Dewsbury	501	Dewsbury	502	Dewsbury	502	Dewsbury
503	Wakefield	503	Wakefield	502	Wakefield	503	Wakefield	503	Wakefield
504	Pontefract	504A	Pontefract	503	Pontefract	504	Pontefract	504	Pontefract
	pt Pontefract	504B	Hemsworth	504	Hemsworth	505	Hemsworth	505	Hemsworth
505	Barnsley	505	Barnsley	505	Barnsley	506	Barnsley	506	Barnsley
506	Wortley	506	Wortley	506	Wortley	507	Wortley	507	Wortley
507	Ecclesall Bierlow	507	Ecclesall Bierlow	507	Ecclesall Bierlow	508	Ecclesall Bierlow	508	Ecclesall Bierlow
508	Sheffield	508	Sheffield	508	Sheffield	509	Sheffield	509	Sheffield
509	Rotherham	509	Rotherham	509	Rotherham	510	Rotherham	510	Rotherham
510	Doncaster	510	Doncaster	510	Doncaster	511	Doncaster	511	Doncaster
511	Thorne	511	Thorne	511	Thorne	512	Thorne	512	Thorne

Place	1851	1861	1871	1881	1891
Goole	512	512	512	513	513
Selby	513	513	513	514	514
Tadcaster	514	514	514	515	515
York	515	515	515	516	516
Pocklington	516	516	516	517	517
Howden	517	517	517	518	518
Beverley	518	518	518	519	519
Sculcoates	519	519	519	520	520
Hull	520	520	520	521	521
Patrington	521	521	521	522	522
Skirlaugh	522	522	522	523	523
Driffield	523	523	523	524	524
Bridlington	524	524	524	525	525
Scarborough	525	525	525	526	526
Malton	526	526	526	527	527
Easingwold	527	527	527	528	528
Thirsk	528	528	528	529	529
Helmsley	529	529	529	530	530
Pickering	530	530	530	531	531
Whitby	531	531	531	532	532
Guisborough	532	532	532	533	533
pt Guisborough	pt Guisborough	pt Guisborough	pt Guisborough		
Middlesbrough				534	534
Stokesley	533	533	533	535	535
Northallerton	534	534	534	536	536
Bedale	535	535	535	537	537
Leyburn	536	536	536	538	538
Askrigg / Aysgarth	537 Askrigg	537 Askrigg	537 Aysgarth	539 Aysgarth	539 Aysgarth
Reeth	538	538	538	540	540
Richmond	539	539	539	541	541

1851	1861	1871	1881	1891
540 Darlington	540 Darlington	540 Darlington	542 Darlington	542 Darlington
541 Stockton	541A Stockton	541 Stockton	543 Stockton	543 Stockton
pt Stockton	541B Hartlepool	542 Hartlepool	544 Hartlepool	544 Hartlepool
542 Auckland	542 Auckland	543 Auckland	545 Auckland	545 Auckland
543 Teesdale	543 Teesdale	544 Teesdale	546 Teesdale	546 Teesdale
544 Weardale	544 Weardale	545 Weardale	547 Weardale	547 Weardale
pt Weardale	pt Weardale	pt Weardale	548 Lanchester	548 Lanchester
545 Durham	545 Durham	546 Durham	549 Durham	549 Durham
546 Easington	546 Easington	547 Easington	550 Easington	550 Easington
547 Houghton le Spring	547 Houghton le Spring	548 Houghton le Spring	551 Houghton le Spring	551 Houghton le Spring
548 Chester le Street	548 Chester le Street	549 Chester le Street	552 Chester le Street	552 Chester le Street
549 Sunderland	549 Sunderland	550 Sunderland	553 Sunderland	553 Sunderland
550 South Shields	550 South Shields	551 South Shields	554 South Shields	554 South Shields
551 Gateshead	551 Gateshead	552 Gateshead	555 Gateshead	555 Gateshead
552 Newcastle upon Tyne	552 Newcastle upon Tyne	553 Newcastle upon Tyne	556 Newcastle upon Tyne	556 Newcastle upon Tyne
553 Tynemouth	553 Tynemouth	554 Tynemouth	557 Tynemouth	557 Tynemouth
554 Castle Ward	554 Castle Ward	555 Castle Ward	558 Castle Ward	558 Castle Ward
555 Hexham	555 Hexham	556 Hexham	559 Hexham	559 Hexham
556 Haltwhistle	556 Haltwhistle	557 Haltwhistle	560 Haltwhistle	560 Haltwhistle
557 Bellingham	557 Bellingham	558 Bellingham	561 Bellingham	561 Bellingham
558 Morpeth	558 Morpeth	559 Morpeth	562 Morpeth	562 Morpeth
559 Alnwick	559 Alnwick	560 Alnwick	563 Alnwick	563 Alnwick
560 Belford	560 Belford	561 Belford	564 Belford	564 Belford
561 Berwick	561 Berwick	562 Berwick	565 Berwick	565 Berwick
562 Glendale	562 Glendale	563 Glendale	566 Glendale	566 Glendale
563 Rothbury	563 Rothbury	564 Rothbury	567 Rothbury	567 Rothbury
564 Alston	564 Alston	565 Alston	568 Alston	568 Alston
565 Penrith	565 Penrith	566 Penrith	569 Penrith	569 Penrith

District	1851	1861	1871	1881	1891
Brampton	566	566	567	570	570
Longtown	567	567	568	571	571
Carlisle	568	568	569	572	572
Wigton	569	569	570	573	573
Cockermouth	570	570	571	574	574
Whitehaven	571	571	572	575	575
Bootle	572	572	573	576	576
East Ward	573	573	574	577	577
West Ward	574	574	575	578	578
Kendal	575	575	576	579	579
Chepstow	576	576	577	580	580
Monmouth	577	577	578	581	581
Abergavenny	578	578A	579	582	582
pt Abergavenny					
Bedwellty		578B	580	583	583
Pontypool	579	579	581	584	584
Newport	580	580	582	585	585
Cardiff	581	581	583	586	586
pt Cardiff					
Pontypridd			584	587	587
Merthyr Tydfil	582	582	585	588	588
Bridgend	583	583	586	589	589
Neath	584	584	587	590	590
pt Neath					
Pontardawe				591	591
Swansea	585	585A	588	592	592
pt Swansea					
Gower		585B	589	593	593
Llanelly	586	586	590	594	594
Llandovery	587	587	591	595	595
Llandilofawr	588	588	592	596	596
Carmarthen	589	589	593	597	597
Narberth	590	590	594	598	598
Pembroke	591	591	595	599	599
Haverfordwest	592	592	596	600	600
Cardigan	593	593	597	601	601

1851	1861	1871	1881	1891
594 Newcastle in Emlyn	594 Newcastle in Emlyn	598 Newcastle in Emlyn	602 Newcastle in Emlyn	602 Newcastle in Emlyn
595 Lampeter	595 Lampeter	599 Lampeter	603 Lampeter	603 Lampeter
596 Aberayron	596 Aberayron	600 Aberayron	604 Aberayron	604 Aberayron
597 Aberystwyth	597 Aberystwyth	601 Aberystwyth	605 Aberystwyth	605 Aberystwyth
598 Tregaron	598 Tregaron	602 Tregaron	606 Tregaron	606 Tregaron
599 Builth	599 Builth	603 Builth	607 Builth	607 Builth
600 Brecknock	600 Brecknock	604 Brecknock	608 Brecknock	608 Brecknock
601 Crickhowell	601 Crickhowell	605 Crickhowell	609 Crickhowell	609 Crickhowell
602 Hay	602 Hay	606 Hay	610 Hay	610 Hay
603 Presteigne	603 Presteigne	607 Presteigne	pt Knighton	pt Knighton
604 Knighton	604 Knighton	608 Knighton	611 Knighton	611 Knighton
605 Rhayader	605 Rhayader	609 Rhayader	612 Rhayader	612 Rhayader
606 Machynlleth	606 Machynlleth	610 Machynlleth	613 Machynlleth	613 Machynlleth
607 Newtown	607 Newtown	611 Newtown	614 Newtown	614 Newtown
608 Montgomery	608 Montgomery	612 Forden	615 Forden	615 Forden
609 Llanfyllin	609 Llanfyllin	613 Llanfyllin	616 Llanfyllin	616 Llanfyllin
610 Holywell	610 Holywell	614 Holywell	617 Holywell	617 Holywell
611 Wrexham	611 Wrexham	615 Wrexham	618 Wrexham	618 Wrexham
612 Ruthin	612 Ruthin	616 Ruthin	619 Ruthin	619 Ruthin
613 St Asaph	613 St Asaph	617 St Asaph	620 St Asaph	620 St Asaph
614 Llanrwst	614 Llanrwst	618 Llanrwst	621 Llanrwst	621 Llanrwst
615 Corwen	615 Corwen	619 Corwen	622 Corwen	622 Corwen
616 Bala	616 Bala	620 Bala	623 Bala	623 Bala
617 Dolgellau	617 Dolgellau	621 Dolgellau	624 Dolgellau	624 Dolgellau
618 Ffestiniog	618 Ffestiniog	622 Ffestiniog	625 Ffestiniog	625 Ffestiniog
619 Pwllheli	619 Pwllheli	623 Pwllheli	626 Pwllheli	626 Pwllheli
620 Caernarfon	620 Caernarfon	624 Caernarfon	627 Caernarfon	627 Caernarfon
621 Bangor	621 Bangor	625 Bangor	628 Bangor	628 Bangor
622 Conway	622 Conway	626 Conway	629 Conway	629 Conway
623 Anglesey	623 Anglesey	627 Anglesey	630 Anglesey	630 Anglesey
pt Anglesey	pt Anglesey	pt Anglesey	pt Anglesey	631 Holyhead

APPENDIX 8 STREET INDEXES 1841

All London registration districts and

RD No	Place	RD No	Place
582	Aberdare	452	Macclesfield
474	Ashton under Lyne	471	Manchester
394	Aston	474	Middleton
329	Bedminster	552	Newcastle upon Tyne
394	Birmingham	234	Norwich
474	Bolton	440	Nottingham
328	Bristol	475	Oldham
469	Bury	452	Prestbury
400	Coventry	475	Prestwich
46	Croydon	96	Portsmouth
469	Deane	476	Radcliffe
328	Dudley	476	Rochdale
474	Eccles	508	Sheffield
394	Edgbaston	105	Southampton
474	Flixton	105	South Stoneham
520	Hull	462	Toxteth Park
499	Leeds	462	West Derby
461	Liverpool		

APPENDIX 9   STREET INDEXES 1851

All London registration districts and

R D No	Place	R D No	Place	R D No	Place
46	Croydon	360	Shrewsbury	481	Chorley
47	Kingston	365	Wellington	482	Preston
54	Medway	367	Stafford	485	Lancaster
57	Tonbridge	371	Stoke on Trent	495	Todmorden
58	Maidstone	379	Wolverhampton	496	Saddleworth
85	Brighton	380	Walsall	497	Huddersfield
92	Chichester	381	West Bromwich	498	Halifax
96	Portsea	382	Dudley	499	Bradford
99	Isle of Wight	383	Stourbridge	500	Hunslet
105	Southampton	384	Kidderminster	501	Leeds
106	South Stoneham	387	Worcester	502	Dewsbury
127	Reading	393	King's Norton	503	Wakefield
134	Brentford	394	Birmingham	506	Wortley
135	Hendon	395	Aston	507	Ecclesall Bierlow
136	Barnet	400	Coventry	508	Sheffield
137	Edmonton	417	Leicester	509	Rotherham
158	Oxford	421	Stamford	515	York
168	Northampton	424	Holbeach	519	Sculcoates
179	Bedford	428	Lincoln	520	Hull
183	Leighton Buzzard	440	Nottingham	531	Whitby
184	Luton	445	Derby	541	Stockton
187	Cambridge	452	Stockport	545	Durham
194	West Ham	453	Macclesfield	549	Sunderland
215	Bury St Edmunds	459	Chester	550	South Shields
222	Ipswich	460A	Wirral	551	Gateshead
228	Yarmouth	460B	Birkenhead	552	Newcastle upon
234	Norwich	461	Liverpool		Tyne
246	King's Lynn	462	West Derby	553	Tynemouth
264	Salisbury	463	Prescot	568	Carlisle
281	St Thomas	465	Wigan	570	Cockermouth
282	Exeter	466	Warrington	578	Abergavenny
287	Plymouth	468	Bolton	580	Newport
288	East Stonehouse	469	Bury	581	Cardiff
289	Stoke Damerel	470	Barton upon Irwell	582	Merthyr Tydfil
316	Bridgwater	471	Chorlton	583	Bridgend
326	Bath	472	Salford	584	Neath
327	Keynsham	473	Manchester	585	Swansea
328	Bedminster	474	Ashton under Lyne	598	Tregaron
329	Bristol	475	Oldham	620	Caernarfon
330	Clifton	476	Rochdale	800	Isle of Man
336	Gloucester	477	Haslingden	900	Jersey
344	Cheltenham	480	Blackburn		

APPENDIX 10   STREET INDEXES 1861 AND 1871

All London registration districts and

1861		1871	
RD No	Place	RD No	Place
46	Croydon	37	Croydon
47	Kingston	38	Kingston
54	Medway	45	Medway
57	Tonbridge	48	Tonbridge
58	Maidstone	49	Maidstone
85	Brighton	76	Brighton
96	Portsea	87	Portsea
105	Southampton	96	Southampton
106	South Stoneham	97	South Stoneham
127	Reading	118	Reading
134	Brentford	125	Brentford
135	Hendon	126	Hendon
137	Edmonton	128	Edmonton
158	Oxford	149	Oxford
168	Northampton	159	Northampton
187	Cambridge	178	Cambridge
194	West Ham	185	West Ham
222	Ipswich	213	Ipswich
228	Yarmouth	219	Yarmouth
234	Norwich	225	Norwich
282	Exeter	272	Exeter
287	Plymouth	277	Plymouth
288	East Stonehouse	278	East Stonehouse
289	Stoke Damerel	279	Stoke Damerel
326	Bath	317	Bath
327	Keynsham	318	Keynsham
328	Bedminster	319	Bedminster
329	Bristol	320	Bristol
330	Clifton	321	Clifton
336	Gloucester	327	Gloucester
344	Cheltenham	335	Cheltenham
371	Stoke on Trent	364	Stoke on Trent
379	Wolverhampton	372	Wolverhampton
381	West Bromwich	374	West Bromwich
382	Dudley	375	Dudley

1861		1871	
RD No	Place	RD No	Place
383	Stourbridge	376	Stourbridge
387	Worcester	380	Worcester
393	King's Norton	386	King's Norton
394	Birmingham	387	Birmingham
395	Aston	388	Aston
400	Coventry	393	Coventry
417	Leicester	410	Leicester
440	Nottingham	433	Nottingham
445	Derby	438	Derby
452	Stockport	445	Stockport
453	Macclesfield	446	Macclesfield
459	Chester	452	Chester
460A	Wirral	453	Wirral
460B	Birkenhead	454	Birkenhead
461	Liverpool	455	Liverpool
462	West Derby	456	West Derby
465	Wigan	459	Wigan
468	Bolton	462	Bolton
469	Bury	463	Bury
470	Barton upon Irwell	464	Barton upon Irwell
471	Chorlton	465	Chorlton
472	Salford	466	Salford
473	Manchester	467	Manchester
474	Ashton under Lyne	468	Ashton under Lyne
475	Oldham	469	Oldham
476	Rochdale	470	Rochdale
477	Haslingden	471	Haslingden
480	Blackburn	474	Blackburn
481	Chorley	475	Chorley
482	Preston	476	Preston
485	Lancaster	479	Lancaster
495	Todmorden	492	Todmorden
496	Saddleworth	493	Saddleworth
497	Huddersfield	494	Huddersfield
498	Halifax	495	Halifax
499	Bradford	496	Bradford

1861		1871	
RD No	Place	RD No	Place
500	Hunslet	497	Hunslet
	pt Hunslet	498	Holbeck
	pt Hunslet	499	Bramley
501	Leeds	500	Leeds
506	Wortley	506	Wortley
507	Ecclesall Bierlow	507	Ecclesall Bierlow
508	Sheffield	508	Sheffield
509	Rotherham	509	Rotherham
515	York	515	York
519	Sculcoates	519	Sculcoates
520	Hull	520	Hull
541A	Stockton	541	Stockton
549	Sunderland	550	Sunderland
550	South Shields	551	South Shields
551	Gateshead	552	Gateshead
552	Newcastle upon Tyne	553	Newcastle upon Tyne
553	Tynemouth	554	Tynemouth
568	Carlisle	569	Carlisle
580	Newport	582	Newport
581	Cardiff	583	Cardiff
582	Merthyr Tydfil	585	Merthyr Tydfil
585A	Swansea	588	Swansea
900	Jersey	900	Jersey

APPENDIX 11 STREET INDEXES 1881 AND 1891

All London registration districts and

1881		1891	
RD No	Place	RD No	Place
30	Epsom	30	Epsom
32	Guildford	32	Guildford
33	Farnham	33	Farnham
38	Croydon	38	Croydon
39	Kingston	39	Kingston
40*	Richmond	40	Richmond
41	Bromley	41	Bromley
42	Dartford	42	Dartford
46	Medway	46	Medway
49	Tonbridge	49	Tonbridge
50	Maidstone	50	Maidstone
62	Thanet	62	Thanet
64*	Dover	64	Dover
65*	Elham	65	Elham
68	Hastings	68	Hastings
70*	Eastbourne	70	Eastbourne
77	Brighton	77	Brighton
78	Steyning	78	Steyning
88	Portsea	88	Portsea
91	Isle of Wight	91	Isle of Wight
93*	Christchurch	93	Christchurch
97	Southampton	97	Southampton
98	South Stoneham	98	South Stoneham
119	Reading	119	Reading
126	Brentford	126	Brentford
127	Hendon	127	Hendon
128*	Barnet	128	Barnet
129	Edmonton	129	Edmonton
142	Wycombe	142	Wycombe
149*	Headington	149*	Headington
150*	Oxford	150*	Oxford
160	Northampton	160	Northampton

*These will not all be available immediately but should appear on the shelves over the next two or three years.

1881		1891	
RD No	Place	RD No	Place
163*	Wellingborough	163	Wellingborough
167	Peterborough	167	Peterborough
171	Bedford	171	Bedford
176*	Luton	176	Luton
179*	Cambridge	179*	Cambridge
186	West Ham	186	West Ham
189*	Romford	189	Romford
213	Ipswich	213	Ipswich
219*	Yarmouth	219	Yarmouth
225	Norwich	225	Norwich
241*	Highworth	241	Highworth
271	St Thomas	271	St Thomas
272*	Exeter	272*	Exeter
273	Newton Abbot	273	Newton Abbot
274*	Totnes	274	Totnes
277	Plymouth	277	Plymouth
278*	East Stonehouse	278*	East Stonehouse
279	Stoke Damerel	279	Stoke Damerel
285*	Barnstaple	285	Barnstaple
300	Redruth	300	Redruth
301	Penzance	301	Penzance
315	Axbridge	315	Axbridge
317	Bath	317	Bath
318*	Keynsham	318*	Keynsham
319	Bedminster	319	Bedminster
320	Bristol	320	Bristol
321	Barton Regis	321	Barton Regis
327	Gloucester	327	Gloucester
329	Stroud	329	Stroud
335	Cheltenham	335	Cheltenham
339	Hereford	339	Hereford
351	Atcham	351	Atcham
362	Wolstanton	362	Wolstanton
363	Stoke on Trent	363	Stoke on Trent
367	Burton upon Trent	367	Burton upon Trent

* These will not all be available immediately but should appear on the shelves over the next two or three years.

1881		1891	
RD No.	Place	RD No.	Place
369*	Lichfield	369	Lichfield
370*	Cannock	370	Cannock
371	Wolverhampton	371	Wolverhampton
372	Walsall	372	Walsall
373	West Bromwich	373	West Bromwich
374	Dudley	374	Dudley
375	Stourbridge	375	Stourbridge
376	Kidderminster	376	Kidderminster
379*	Worcester	379	Worcester
385	King's Norton	385	King's Norton
386	Birmingham	386	Birmingham
387	Aston	387	Aston
392	Coventry	392	Coventry
395	Warwick	395	Warwick
409	Leicester	409	Leicester
420	Lincoln	420	Lincoln
424	Caistor	424	Caistor
425	Glanford Brigg	425	Glanford Brigg
429	Mansfield	429	Mansfield
430	Basford	430	Basford
431	Nottingham	431	Nottingham
435	Shardlow	435	Shardlow
436	Derby	436	Derby
437	Belper	437	Belper
439	Chesterfield	439	Chesterfield
443	Stockport	443	Stockport
444	Macclesfield	444	Macclesfield
445	Altrincham	445	Altrincham
446*	Runcorn	446	Runcorn
447	Northwich	447	Northwich
449	Nantwich	449	Nantwich
450	Chester	450	Chester
451*	Wirral	451*	Wirral
452	Birkenhead	452	Birkenhead
453	Liverpool	453	Liverpool

* These will not all be available immediately but should appear on the shelves over the next two or three years.

1881		1891	
RD No	Place	RD No	Place
454	Toxteth Park	454*	Toxteth Park
455	West Derby	455	West Derby
456	Prescott	456	Prescott
457	Ormskirk	457	Ormskirk
458	Wigan	458	Wigan
459	Warrington	459	Warrington
460	Leigh	460	Leigh
461	Bolton	461	Bolton
462	Bury	462	Bury
463	Barton upon Irwell	463	Barton upon Irwell
464	Chorlton	464	Chorlton
465	Salford	465	Salford
466	Manchester	466	Manchester
467	Prestwich	467	Prestwich
468	Ashton under Lyne	468	Ashton under Lyne
469	Oldham	469	Oldham
470	Rochdale	470	Rochdale
471	Haslingden	471	Haslingden
472	Burnley	472	Burnley
474	Blackburn	474	Blackburn
475	Chorley	475	Chorley
476	Preston	476	Preston
477	Fylde	477	Fylde
479	Lancaster	479	Lancaster
481	Ulverston	481	Ulverston
482	Barrow in Furness	482	Barrow in Furness
491	Wharfedale	491	Wharfedale
492	Keighley	492	Keighley
493*	Todmorden	493*	Todmorden
494*	Saddleworth	494*	Saddleworth
495	Huddersfield	495	Huddersfield
496	Halifax	496	Halifax
497	Bradford	497	Bradford
498	Hunslet	498	Hunslet
499*	Holbeck	499*	Holbeck

* These will not all be available immediately but should appear on the shelves over the next two or three years.

1881		1891	
RD No	Place	RD No	Place
500	Bramley	500	Bramley
501	Leeds	501	Leeds
502	Dewsbury	502	Dewsbury
503	Wakefield	503	Wakefield
504	Pontefract	504	Pontefract
506	Barnsley	506	Barnsley
507	Wortley	507	Wortley
508	Ecclesall Bierlow	508	Ecclesall Bierlow
509	Sheffield	509	Sheffield
510	Rotherham	510	Rotherham
511	Doncaster	511	Doncaster
516	York	516	York
520	Sculcoates	520	Sculcoates
521	Hull	521	Hull
526	Scarborough	526	Scarborough
533	Guisborough	533	Guisborough
534	Middlesbrough	534	Middlesbrough
542	Darlington	542	Darlington
543	Stockton	543	Stockton
544	Hartlepool	544	Hartlepool
545	Auckland	545	Auckland
548	Lanchester	548	Lanchester
549	Durham	549	Durham
550	Easington	550	Easington
552	Chester le Street	552	Chester le Street
553	Sunderland	553	Sunderland
554	South Shields	554	South Shields
555	Gateshead	555	Gateshead
556	Newcastle upon Tyne	556	Newcastle upon Tyne
557	Tynemouth	557	Tynemouth
562*	Morpeth	562	Morpeth
572	Carlisle	572	Carlisle
574	Cockermouth	574	Cockermouth
575	Whitehaven	575	Whitehaven
579	Kendal	579	Kendal

* These will not all be available immediately but should appear on the shelves over the next two or three years.

1881		1891	
RD No	Place	RD No	Place
583	Bedwellty	583	Bedwellty
584	Pontypool	584	Pontypool
585	Newport	585	Newport
586	Cardiff	586	Cardiff
587	Pontypridd	587	Pontypridd
588	Merthyr Tydfil	588	Merthyr Tydfil
589*	Bridgend	589	Bridgend
590	Neath	590	Neath
592	Swansea	592	Swansea
594	Llanelly	594	Llanelly
617	Holywell	617	Holywell
618	Wrexham	618	Wrexham
627	Caernarfon	627	Caernarfon
900*	Jersey	900*	Jersey

* These will not all be available immediately but should appear on the shelves over the next two or three years.

APPENDIX 12 PLACES STREET INDEXED IN PART

(available on officer's desk only)

1841	1851	1861	1871	1881
	Biggleswade			Ashby de la Zouch
	Cheadle			Barnes
	Congleton			
Bedford	Coppenhall			
Dunstable		Dunstable	Dunstable	Dunstable
				East Sheen
				Finedon
Horsham	Hereford	Horsham	Horsham	Hereford
	Horsham			Horsham
				Kettering
				Loughborough
	Knutsford			
	Leominster			
	Leamington			
Leighton Buzzard	Lowestoft	Leighton Buzzard	Leighton Buzzard	Leighton Buzzard
Lowestoft		Lowestoft	Lowestoft	Lowestoft
Luton		Luton	Luton	Luton
				Mortlake
				Petworth
Petworth	Melton Mowbray	Petworth	Petworth	
	Petworth			
	Radford			
	Runcorn			Richmond
Stapleton	Stapleton	Stapleton	Salisbury	Stapleton
		Tewkesbury	Stapleton	

APPENDIX 13   BIBLIOGRAPHY

E J Higgs, *Making Sense of the Census: The Manuscript Returns for England and Wales, 1801-1901,* HMSO, 1989.

Susan Lumas, *An Introduction to...The Census Returns of England and Wales,* FFHS, 1992.

Ray Wiggins, *St Catherine's House Districts,* privately printed, Northwood, no date.

J S W Gibson, *Census Returns 1841-1881 on Microfilm: A Directory to Local Holdings,* 5th edn, FFHS, 1990.

J S W Gibson and Colin Chapman, *Census Indexes and Indexing,* FFHS, 1983.

J S W Gibson and M Medlycott, *Local Census Listings 1522-1930, Holdings in the British Isles* , FFHS, 1992

J S W Gibson, *Marriage, Census and other Indexes for Family Historians,* FFHS, 1992.

John M Boreham, *The Census and How to Use it,* Essex Society for Family History, 1982.

Andrew Todd, *Basic Sources for Family History: Back to the early 1880s,* Bury, Lancs, 1989.

C R Chapman, *Pre 1841 Censuses and Population Listings*, Lockin Publishing, 1991.

Alan Godfrey, *Old Ordnance Survey Maps,* Gateshead, various dates.

George Pelling, *Beginning Your Family History,* 5th edn, FFHS, 1990.

M E Bryant Rosier, *Index to Census Registration Districts,* FFHS, 1990.

Frederick Engels, *The Condition of the Working Class in England*, Chapter III, p 30, ed W O Henderson and W H Chaloner, 2nd edn, Chapter III, p 30, Basil Blackwell, 1971.

Gordon Johnson, *Census Records for Scottish Families,* Association of Scottish Family History Societies, Aberdeen, 1990.

Heraldic Artists Ltd, *Handbook on Irish Genealogy,* Heraldic Artists Ltd, 1978.

Donald F Begley, *Irish Genealogy: A Record Finder,* Heraldic Artists Ltd, 1981.

People and Places in the Victorian Census: a review and bibliography of publications based substantially on the manuscript Census Enumerators' Books 1841-1911. Dennis Mills and Carol Pearce (comp), Institute of British Geographers, Historical Geography Research Series No 23, November 1989.

The Phillimore Atlas and Index of Parish Registers, ed Cecil R Humphery-Smith, Phillimore, 1984.

Population of Each County of Great Britain: 1841, (sessional papers I, House of Commons, Vol II, paper no 52, 277).

Population Tables I: Numbers of the inhabitants: Vol I: 1852-1853, (sessional papers, House of Commons, Vol LXXXV, paper no 1631).

Population Tables I: Numbers of the inhabitants: Vol II: 1852-1853, (sessional papers, House of Commons, Vol LXXXVI, paper no 1632.

Population Tables I: Numbers and Distribution of the People: 1862, (sessional papers, House of Commons, Vol L, paper no 3056).

Population Tables: Area, Houses and Inhabitants: Vol I, Counties: 1872, (sessional papers, House of Commons, Vol LXVI, paper no c.671-I, Part I).

Population Tables: Area, Houses and Inhabitants: Vol II, Registration or Union Counties: 1872 (sessional papers, House of Commons, Vol LXVI, paper no c.676-I, Part II, 1).

Population Tables: Area, Houses and Population: Counties: 1883 (sessional papers, House of Commons, Vol LXXVIII, paper no c.3562, 1).

Population Tables: Registration Counties:1883 (sessional papers, House of Commons, Vol LXXIX, paper no c.3563, 1).